C000265426

COLEEN GREENWOOD AND KAREN CREAR

Healing From The Burns

Life after Fireman Scam

C R E A R
PUBLISHING
EST 2023

First edition

ISBN: 978-1-7392765-6-0

"Each time a woman stands up for herself, without knowing it possibly, she stands up for all women"

MAYA ANGELOU

Contents

Foreword

A portion of proceeds from sales of this book will be donated to Women's Aid.

www.womensaid.org.uk

Preface

Witness Impact Statement written by Coleen Greenwood in the weeks following Greg's disappearance, which was read aloud in Court by the Prosecuting Barrister on sentencing day, prior to Greg Wilson being handed a six-year prison sentence.

"It's been more than five years since James Scott first came into my life, and three years since his lies and manipulation started to unravel.

Saturday 25th February 2017 should have been my wedding day at Wynyard Hall. Instead, after being confronted with the truth, James deserted me and our child, handing him through a window to my daughter and driving off, saying he would only be a minute. Our baby and I haven't seen him since.

The shock, hurt and disbelief I've felt from this day is extremely hard to put into words. It felt like it was happening to someone else.

The complete devastation to discover that my whole life and plans for the future were built on deceit and lies is heartbreaking. The following days I found it almost impossible to carry on and I barely ate or slept. The minimal sleep I did get was filled with horrendous nightmares.

As time progressed and the reality set in that James Scott, the man I loved, never existed, felt to me like a bereavement.

These emotions were counterbalanced by the increasing feeling of stupidity and humiliation I felt.

Telephone calls and letters arrived chasing debts that James had incurred, and I found myself explaining the situation over and over again. This was embarrassing and I felt to the outside world that I was a complete and utter gullible fool.

I have children from a previous relationship and felt like my family was complete. James decided to have a vasectomy as I was fearful of falling pregnant again.

James told me he attended hospital to have this done. I saw him after the operation and saw bruising and dressings on his penis. I was also shown a medical report which stated he now had a nil sperm count.

Two months after seeing this report I fell pregnant again. The feelings of horror and disbelief were staggering, and I couldn't comprehend how it could have happened.

I was actually horrified that people would think I'd been un-faithful. James on the other hand took the news well, saying that there was a one in 200 chance of pregnancy after a vasectomy. We continued with the pregnancy which caused me many health complications.

My waters broke at 23 weeks and when I delivered our baby, I needed an emergency C section. I nearly died during this and my baby was put on a life support machine. We were told his health had deteriorated and there was a chance he wouldn't make it.

This, all added to the trauma for me to know James faked the vasectomy risking mine and our baby's life, sickens me to the stomach. The thought that my two older daughters could have been left without a mother is horrifying. To be manipulated to this extent by James is something I will never be able to come to terms with.

I'm not the same person I was before James came into my life. I believed I was sharing my life with a wonderful, caring man, a true hero who risked his life as a firefighter.

I heard a story of James jumping out of the window of a burning building with a small child, saving his life and breaking his own back during the fall. I even saw a thank you card from the boy, and texts of gratitude from the child's parents.

To learn these are all lies, and James was never a firefighter shows what a devious and manipulative person he is. I now find it hard to trust my own instincts and always over analyse situations.

I worry this has made me cynical and unapproachable to people, but I can't control these feelings. I also left my job during this deception, which has knocked my confidence and status.

Finding out that James was a fraud was a huge blow to me. Added to this fact that he defrauded my sister out of a huge amount of money, put a huge strain on our relationship.

I've seen her struggle both financially and emotionally and despite this, she still managed to look after me through these awful times. My two daughters regarded James as a stepdad and a friend.

To find out they had also been part of the fraud and manipulation was horrendous. It's horrible to see my daughters lose trust in people.

The whole fraud has created long-lasting effects on mine and my family's lives. I continue to suffer from anxiety and still have difficulty sleeping. I experience incidents where I believe I see James in everyday life.

Looking to the future, the consequences of what James did to us is complicated. Our child's birth certificate has a father's name that never existed, and I've found no way of changing it.

One of the hardest things I will have to do is, at some point in the future, sit down with my wonderful son and explain the horrendous truth about his father's deception.

This is a task I wouldn't wish on anyone. This will have to be done with the tremendous support I have received from my lovely *family, whose support I couldn't have done without through this devastating time in my life."*

1

Sentencing Day

Sentencing day – 8th April 2020

Facebook Messenger received 18:24 from an unknown number.

"...Hi Coleen, I hope you don't mind me messaging you, but I've just seen the news. I'm in a relationship with Greg, and he's been phoning me from prison. We're engaged and he's supposed to be taking me to Dubai next week..."

The noise around me faded to a hum as time seemed to stop in that very moment. The sickening realisation that despite my misplaced naïve hopes that Greg Wilson would have stopped, taken stock of the hurt he had caused, the lies and damage inflicted on so many, somehow in those months following his guilty plea in court he would have resolved to change his ways. But no, he was up to his old tricks again. Another poor woman being gaslit and manipulated from the confines of his prison cell.

I really felt for this poor stranger. The gut-wrenching despair she must have felt upon turning the news on that evening, to see her fiancé emblazoned across the screen. The list of his heartless crimes for the whole world to digest. And her life, just as mine had been, blown apart in a split second. Discovering that everything she knew was a lie. I took a deep breath, running my fingers through my shoulder length blonde hair. With my hand shaking, I slowly dialled my twin sister Karen's number. I so wanted to help this poor woman but knew deep down I just wasn't strong enough yet. I honestly didn't know if I would ever be strong enough.

After a few rings Karen answered the call, her voice bright and breezy. She sounded in high spirits, no doubt a little tipsy after the congratulatory drinks her and my brother-in-law Ryan would have enjoyed that afternoon. It had been a lovely warm day, and I could just imagine the two of them in their little 'yarden' raising a glass to the verdict. They may have had to downsize to a more modest home and forfeit having a garden, but my sister had made the best of the limited space they now had. It was a little oasis of pot plants and a fragrant herb garden. She always did try to make the best of a bad situation.

"How are you holding up Col?" she questioned me, her voice sounding light and carefree. "You must feel that a real weight has been lifted from you, I certainly know I do. Six years, that's a hell of a lot of lumpy porridge that old Greg is going to have to eat. I hope it flipping chokes him." She gave a slow, resigned sigh, her voice taking on a more sombre edge. "Thank God it is finally all over for us all. It's been hell but at least we got our justice, and he is where he is meant to be – behind bars."

I sank further back into my chair, almost wishing I could disappear into it completely, and sighed deeply, not wanting to sully her happy mood but needing to tell her about the message. My fingers nervously plucked at a loose thread from the sofa cushion. When I was anxious, I could never keep my hands still and would fidget for Britain. "I wish that were true Karen, but I think the next chapter is just starting. And unfortunately, we're a long way from it all being over. I fear there's much more still to come."

Even over the phone I could hear my sister's sharp intake of breath. The clock on my fireplace ticked ominously as the seconds passed excruciatingly slowly without her uttering a single word. I knew in my heart she was frightened to discover what I had. Hoping beyond hope that Greg Wilson was well and truly behind us and could be resigned forever to our family's history books. It seemed an eternity but, in all probability, only a few seconds had passed when she eventually spoke.

"Why, what is it? What's happened now?"

I read aloud the message I had received from the unknown woman, still hardly believing it myself. But then again, why was I surprised? Nothing Greg did should surprise me anymore.

"Will you ring her Karen?" I asked my sister, hating the neediness in my voice. But I just couldn't face speaking to another one of Greg's victims. It was all just too raw.

Karen sighed slowly. "Yes, leave it with me. The poor woman needs to know everything about her 'fiancé'". She let out a slow bitter laugh. "Poor thing. She's in for one hell of a shock."

As I waited for my sister to call back, I tried to keep myself busy and started making biscuits for Charlie – chocolate chip, his favourites. Anything to try and get my mind off Greg. I knew dwelling on him wasn't a healthy thing for me to do. But I couldn't help but fret and as I sat waiting to hear from Karen the time slowly ebbed away. The baking cookies in the oven, long-forgotten.

My smoke alarm sounding furiously in my ears pulled me back into the here and now. I was pulling the black, incinerated biscuits out of my oven when my mobile phone began to ring.

It was Karen. I dropped the baking tray on the floor, not caring that the burnt biscuits scattered all over the tiles. My heart was in my mouth as I accepted the call and listened to what Karen had to say. She had spoken at length to the woman. Told her everything about Greg, tore her whole world apart, like ours had been on so many occasions.

The woman had initially been quite optimistic talking to my sister, naively hoping she would be able to reassure her, sure that there must have been some sort of terrible mix up, not understanding why the love of her life would be on the national news. Surely there must be some sort of mistake? As Karen talked to her, any optimism the woman had felt in the beginning fizzled out to nothing, like a flame being snuffed out.

Greg had spun her quite the tale. Told her he was in prison on a minor tax issue, some administration problem from when he had been in the Army. It was all a big misunderstanding of course, which was being cleared up as they spoke. He should never have been in prison and heads would roll because of it. He had informed her he was due to be released at the weekend and not to worry, he would be out in good time to take her to Dubai the following week.

She had had the wool well and truly pulled over her eyes by Greg. However, no one knew better than me just how plausible and convincing a liar that man could be.

He had spoken to her the words she longed to hear – that she was the love of his life, how he couldn't exist without her by his side and that she was his soul mate, the other half that made him whole. I kept silent as she told me. He had said all those words to me too. Words I had cherished but now know they were all empty promises.

As I listened to Karen, slowly absorbing her words, I couldn't help but pull my thick woollen jumper more tightly around me as a shiver of revulsion crept over my entire body. He was telling this woman so many, many lies. Making her believe that she was his world, all while he still had his girlfriend patiently waiting for him during his incarceration. The poor young woman who had sat loyally by his side in court, had believed he was a good man deep down, who had simply made mistakes. A man wholly capable of redemption who had learnt his lesson and would turn his life around. No, all Greg Wilson had learnt was new ways to manipulate women. I wondered if the woman who had messaged me was his only other love interest or were there countless other females dotted around the country believing they had met the man of their dreams? I didn't know, but what I did know was that he was nobody's Prince Charming. No, he truly was the stuff of your worst nightmares.

Once I finished the telephone conversation and reassured my sister I would be okay, I headed upstairs. I really needed an early night. The truth was I just wanted to sleep, for this day to be well and truly over. The day I had been waiting so long for, to see Greg pay for his crimes, but it had ended on such a sour note. Once in bed I pulled the covers over my head so I could hide away from the world. I had a very bad feeling in the pit of my stomach. A feeling I hoped I had left in the past.

2

Love And Lies

That night it didn't matter how many sheep I counted jumping over little fences, there was no possibility of any sleep. I stared at my bedroom ceiling as the ominous darkness gave way to eventual daylight and my mind was in turmoil. Realistically I shouldn't have even felt surprised, let alone the raft of emotions that were presently engulfing me. I was by now only too aware what type of man I had been in love with. My "James" was not the faithful loving man who he had always claimed to be. A man who would never even contemplate being unfaithful, who found the notion completely abhorrent. Only ever having had two sexual partners before we became an item, or so he had told me. This I now know is utter rubbish. In the years that followed the end of our relationship I had been told on many, many occasions what sort of man my 'James' really was. A man incapable of keeping it in his trousers. There had of course been his double life of cheating when he had been in a relationship with me and his wife Rachel simultaneously. But there had also been many more infidelities prior to this time, both whilst he was with Rachel in their early days together, and no doubt whilst he had been with me too. I wonder now if he had always been sniffing around anything in a skirt like a randy chihuahua. I doubt in my heart whether he had ever been faithful to me during our two-and-a-half-year relationship.

Rachel had filled me in on all of Greg's other women when they had been together. How she had made allowances for him repeatedly, believed his lies as he promised that it would never happen again. Desperately begging her for another chance, pleading with her how their sons needed their father and how much he adored her and his family. But invariably it happened again. He would be good for a while, playing the doting father and faithful husband, but then the lure of the fairer sex would just be too great for him to resist. She had told me during one of our lengthy telephone conversations how, years earlier, she had set up her own little business. She had been incredibly proud to rent a modest shop outlet in the town centre in Darlington, selling her bespoke, handmade jewellery. A hobby she had started whilst Greg had been in the Army and the family had been posted overseas in Germany. She had an artistic flair and was talented and had hoped it would prove a lucrative and rewarding endeavour for her and their family.

Rachel had taken her sons out shopping one afternoon in Darlington city centre. They had been assisted in one store by an attractive younger woman who was working as a shop assistant and was wearing a necklace that Rachel had instantly recognised as one she had made herself. Rachel had been delighted to see her handiwork around the neck of the other woman and had proudly informed her that her necklace was one of her pieces and how lovely it looked on her. The young woman had received the compliment with a shy, happy smile and informed Rachel that it had been a romantic gift from her doting boyfriend Greg. Rachel had felt an icy shiver make its way down her spine as the prickle of suspicion suddenly took hold. She didn't want to assume the worst, but no one knew better than her how unfaithful her husband had been in the past. Trying to keep her composure in check, Rachel had calmly questioned the woman more about her generous boyfriend. It soon became clear that the Greg the shop assistant spoke so fondly of was none other than Rachel's Greg too. Her husband had been cheating yet again. He had pinched the necklace that Rachel had so lovingly and painstakingly made, then passed it on to his sidepiece. What a generous man her philandering spouse could be!

His light-fingered habit of taking possessions and passing them on to his new love interest had come into play in our relationship too. After Rachel and I had made a connection, we had become Facebook friends, and so, as to be expected, we had both had a good old stalk of each other's accounts. It hurt us both to see the other woman with 'our man'. But we were both desperate to discover what 'our' man had really been up to. One of my posts had been when I was heavily pregnant with Charlie. It was New Year's Eve and back then I couldn't do much celebrating at all, spending most of my days in bed. But on this occasion, as it was a special day, I had made the effort and had got dressed up as much as I could – not easy considering I was pretty much spherical by that point. I was wearing a stretchy velvet dress adorned with a lovely sparkly gold necklace that James had given me earlier that day. However, now it transpired it had not been his to give away. After seeing the necklace proudly worn around my neck in the photo, Rachel had dashed to her bedroom with her heart in her mouth and begun frantically searching through her treasured jewellery box. As she had feared, her necklace, the one she rarely wore as she liked to keep for best, had gone. She was devastated. Greg had given her that necklace as a love token many years before and he had obviously thought so little of her feelings that he had re-gifted it to me. I felt so badly for her. It was not as if I could even return the jewellery to her. In all likelihood she wouldn't have wanted it back anyway, but it was long gone. Anything that had been given to me by 'James' had been donated to the local charity shop after he had run off. I'm sure the charity shop would have made a good profit on the necklace as it really was quite beautiful. Whether they would have managed to sell all his garish golf jumpers and skinny jeans? Well, that was another matter.

Iain, Greg's brother-in-law, had also filled in the dots about my erstwhile ex's philandering. A few years before we met, he had been on a lad's night out with Greg and others. Greg himself never really seemed to have that many friends of his own and liked to latch on to Iain and his mates whenever he could. Greg had gone to the bar as it was his round and was about to pay for the drinks. However, when he reached into his pocket to pull out some money, a SIM card had come flying out and landed just by Iain's feet. Greg had pounced quickly to retrieve it, but Iain had been too quick for him. As he picked up the dropped SIM, he suspiciously questioned Greg about it. This was the days before dual SIM phones existed, when swapping SIMs appeared very dodgy indeed and, at least to a faithful man like Iain, would only mean one thing – Greg was cheating on his sister yet again. Of course, Greg was full of explanations and excuses and as always was extremely convincing. Iain, recounting the story to us though, remembered how he knew in the pit of his stomach that it was all lies. A guilty look, albeit fleeting, had flashed across Greg's face before he had managed to get his emotions in check. He told us that all his family believed Greg to be a two-timing snake who couldn't be trusted. But there was no convincing Rachel and she wanted to hear none of it. She knew what her husband was like, but she continued to stick by her man through thick and thin. Loyal to the end.

Years later whilst in a relationship with me, I know for definite that Greg had cheated on me. Of course, I didn't know at the time. To me he was pretty much perfect back then. No, it would take years until I would finally discover the truth. I had been busy working one Thursday afternoon whilst Greg had been looking after baby Charlie. He had been spotted walking brazenly around the Metro Centre shops, arm in arm with an attractive younger brunette woman who was pushing Charlie in his pram. My Charlie, my son. But looking to all and sundry like a happy family unit out for an afternoon of shopping with their newborn gurgling away happily. It was Lee Walker. The successful businessman whose identity Greg had once stolen. Lee spotted Greg and his companion coming out of an upscale women's boutique weighed down by countless shopping bags. Not doubt Greg was giving this lucky lady the 'Pretty Woman' treatment too. Lee had been doing some last-minute shopping with his wife and had literally bumped straight into the pair as they headed into the shop. Lee, who by this point knew all about Greg's impersonating him, had confronted the couple angrily, and rightly so, wanting some answers. But as always, Greg had managed to scurry away like a scared little rabbit and disappeared, with his lady friend and Charlie, amongst the sea of frantic shoppers.

I only discovered this altercation upon meeting Lee for the

first time a year or so after this encounter. It makes me feel so sad to realise that, as I had sat at work that afternoon, in blissful ignorance, working hard and counting the hours down until I could see my fiancé and baby again, spending a lovely, relaxed evening together, my fiancé had been out with another woman. I'm still staggered by how unashamedly he could flaunt his lies and indiscretions so publicly. To this day I don't know who that young woman at the shopping centre with him was. I just hope that she is ok and not another one of his many victims, left devastated and damaged by knowing and loving the man.

Greg always liked to take risks. He loved to feel he was always the cleverest person in any room, forever invincible. I really think he got a kick out of the thrill of knowing that discovery could always be a mere moment away.

3

A Mother's Love

During the three years it had taken for Greg's case to be heard in court, I had healed. It hadn't been easy. I can't lie or be flippant about it. I am undoubtedly a very different person now. How could I not be? Not quite as trusting and open as I once was. But with the help of my lovely family and friends we had all gone on to rebuild our lives. Choosing not to be defined by the destruction he had caused.

I wanted to be the bigger person. Show that, despite what had happened to me, I could somehow rise above it all. Although Maureen was Greg's mother, I knew that, unlike her son, she was guilty of no crimes. She was Charlie's Grandmother and as such they both deserved to know each other better. To build a relationship. I knew how important Grandparents were in children's lives and I wasn't going to be a barrier to my son getting to know his.

It was early March 2017 a couple of weeks after Greg had run off and I had invited Maureen and John to come to my home. They did come twice, and it was lovely to see them. They were a nice, down-to-earth couple and very unassuming. They were absolutely nothing like Greg had described them and were clearly very fond of Charlie. They generously brought flowers for me, and a gingerbread man and crayons for Charlie. They helped to piece together the early life of Greg and enabled me to know the man I thought I knew.

Maureen was extremely hurt by what her son had done, but she clearly still loved him despite everything. As a mother myself I know how difficult it would be to turn your back on your own child. She suggested I made a scrapbook for Charlie with pictures in it of his father, so that my son wouldn't forget her son. This would allow Charlie, in the future, to put a face to the name Greg Wilson. I had smiled at her politely and bitten down hard on my tongue so I wouldn't speak my truth. I was happy to see Maureen and John, to encourage a close bond between them and Charlie, however I had no desire to make a book to remind Charlie of the existence of his biological father. The father that had deceived us all, run away from his son, denied his very existence. The man who had fled and never looked back. No, that was a step too far, even for me.

Looking at Maureen's pale, concerned face that afternoon, pausing from time to time to take a pressed handkerchief from her cardigan pocket to stem the tears spilling from her eyes, I was staggered just how far this woman was from the picture Greg had painted of his mother. The cold, hard-faced, business driven matriarch he had had to endure throughout his childhood. Her tired, lined face and timid countenance triggered a memory in me from a night over a year earlier. Seeing Maureen interact with Charlie, tickling her grandson's feet lovingly to make him giggle, made the memory even more laughable. Greg had once again been playing the generous host.

He had invited ten family members and friends to Sunderland Football stadium as his guests to watch a game. Not in the stands of course, that would be far too humble for Greg. Oh no, they were all being treated to a private box with all food and drinks included. My sister, Karen had reluctantly accepted the invitation and attended with Ryan, neither of them being football fans but touched by his generosity. Karen never for a single second thinking that she would be the one unknowingly footing the bill for such a lavish event.

It had been a lovely evening for everyone. Although Karen and I were not really into the football, we had enjoyed getting stuck into the food and drinks, chatting and relaxing whilst everyone else enjoyed the game. There was much anticipation in the stadium that night. It was a special game; Sunderland was playing against Chelsea and little Bradley Lowery, a local six-year-old boy who was battling cancer, was taking a goal kick for his beloved team, Sunderland. The crowd had been on their feet in celebration when Bradley scored the goal.

There was a happy, convivial atmosphere in our private box too. There had been far too much food, but everyone had enjoyed what they had had. I had pushed my chair away from the table and began collecting and stacking up everyone's dirty plates. I thought it would help the waiting staff out a little and would make it more comfortable for us all to have the dirty dishes moved away from where we were sitting. As I busied myself with this task, carrying a stack of side plates, I was stopped abruptly in my tracks by Greg's furious voice reverberating around the room. Everyone instantly fell silent as their heads turned towards him to stare in shock.

"For God's sake Coleen, what the hell do you think you are doing?"

I slowly turned to face him, as shocked as everyone else clearly was. His face had turned a disconcerting shade of red and there was a little vein throbbing at his temple.

I was frozen to the spot, the pile of plates still in my hands, perilously close to sliding out of my grasp. What had I done wrong? I really couldn't understand why he was so angry with me. I could feel my eyes start to fill up with tears and my cheeks prickled with embarrassment. Everyone was looking at us, clearly clueless as to what the issue was, why 'James' was so annoyed and just as eager to discover why.

"There are staff to do that for us," Greg shouted. "We don't clear away our own mess, it's not the done thing. My mother would be absolutely horrified to see you clearing all our plates away like that. You always need to realise your standing in life. I'm telling you now Col, when you meet Mum, you best not show me up like this. I would be so embarrassed."

The stunned silence in the room made the situation seem even more humiliating for me. I was mortified at the way Greg had shouted at me; it was so unlike him. More than that I was appalled by how pompous and entitled he sounded. Karen, sensing my crippling discomfort, quickly tried to restore the previous happy atmosphere and get everyone chatting again. Despite her best efforts the feeling of awkwardness was still evident in everyone.

All I wanted to do in that moment was run away and hide. Lock myself away in the ladies' toilet and have a good old cry. Was he so scared of his mother's disapproval in me that he thought it was ok to shout at me like that? I was his fiancée, but he had chosen to humiliate me in front of our family and close friends. At that point if I hadn't already been nervous about meeting Maureen, I sure as hell was now. What a scary, opinionated dragon of a woman she sounded. Greg always said she was a bit of a ballbreaker in business, but she sounded like an insufferable snob too.

There were other memories about his mother that still circulated in my mind. Times when he had endeavoured to make her appear a warmer kinder version of herself. These instances would tend to revolve around Charlie. At one of my many prenatal appointments to check Charlie's development she had requested a copy of the printout from the monitor tracking his heartbeat. She wanted to use this to have a bespoke picture made to hang in her office which she was going to title 'Little Miracle' so she would always have him there with her.

Also, after Charlie's traumatic birth, she decided to donate a generous sum of money to the Neonatal department at Newcastle RVI Hospital so that they could purchase a new much needed incubator. Greg had shown me messages that Maureen had supposedly received, kind words of gratitude from the RVI. I had been touched by her kind gesture. My heart had begun to soften towards my formidable Mother-in-law. She couldn't be all bad. Of course it was all lies. No new incubator. No new piece of artwork for her office wall.

I dragged myself back to the present and as I looked across my living room to the 'real' Maureen, sitting in front of me on a comfortable armchair, sipping slowly on her tea. She was so polite and unassuming, even offering to put the kettle on for me as she was worried I was tired, caring for Charlie on my own. Most definitely nothing like the mother Greg had so often described. A woman expecting staff to do menial tasks, imagining herself too good for such things. This real Maureen was a good woman, a woman keen to help. Heartbroken by the actions of her son but clearly still with a mother's love in her heart for him. It was despicable that he would concoct another version of his own mother to people. People who she would never get to meet but would believe her to be the polar opposite of who she actually was. He felt absolutely no remorse in lying about the woman who had given him life. This just proved that no one was safe from his deceit.

Maureen and John visited Charlie at my home on two occasions in total. They had been convivial meetings, very pleasant and with no arguments or disagreements whatsoever. However, after the second visit they left and never returned. I still don't understand why they never contacted us again. I choose to believe in my heart that it was just too difficult for Maureen, knowing what her own son had done, how hard my life had become because of him. I think she must have decided the kindest thing was to leave us be. Take a step back from us all. Whatever her motivations were, the door is always open to her. If she ever feels she would like to reconnect with her grandson, I would be happy to see this become a reality. I would never hold her responsible for her son's actions.

4

To Trust Again

Time really can be the most wonderful healer. Prior to sentencing day, and the fallout from it, I was living a much happier and contented life in a sleepy village in the tranquil Yorkshire Dales. I had moved there from Chester-Le-Street several months earlier. It had been an awful wrench to move away from my girls, Laura and Katie. They were both adults now and firmly resisted my attempts to have them relocate to the country with us. They much preferred the hustle and bustle of a big city, the shopping, nightlife. They didn't want to give that up. But the distance between us didn't diminish our close bond in the slightest. To this day I still enjoy daily telephone calls with my girls, and we meet up at least a couple of times a month.

Life had felt a million miles away from the whirlwind of life with Greg. I was happy, much more so now that he was safely behind bars for the next few years and, as I believed, incapable of hurting anyone else. Happiness is never something that should be taken for granted.

In time I had let my barriers down, eventually had gone on

to entrust my heart to someone else. I had dared to love again. I started to date Scott. Only occasional dates to start with, but in time they became more frequent. He was a divorced dad of two young sons. A decent, honest, hardworking guy and a really lovely man. One of the most patient and easy-going people you could ever wish to meet. Our relationship had started tentatively, me preferring, for many months, to just remain friends. I kept him at arm's length, fearful of being burnt in a relationship again. Scott waited in the wings patiently and our romance developed over time. And three years after Greg's disappearance we even married in an intimate little ceremony, with just Karen, Ryan and my girls as witnesses. It was a far cry from the huge wedding that Greg had promised me, but it was perfect. At least this one was real!

Back In the early days of our relationship I would question Scott on absolutely everything, though. I couldn't help it. I would look for problems where there were none. I had to meet every one of his family and friends within a few weeks of meeting him. I would check every minute detail he would tell me, constantly worried I was being deceived once again. Even on our first date, I made a point to check the name on his bank card when he was paying for our drinks. I did it surreptitiously, constantly checking he wasn't looking at me, so he didn't realise what I was up to. I felt relief in seeing his name printed in little letters on his card correspond with what he had told me. This further reassured me Scott was not like Greg.

Despite my reticence, Scott eventually put the pieces of my broken heart back together. Charlie, no longer a baby, was now four years old. Along with Scott's two sons and our two mad rescue moggies, Tiddles and Dave, we were all happy.

Together, Scott and I made the decision to start the process for Scott to legally adopt Charlie. This would make our little family complete. Scott is my rock. His love and support for me makes me stronger day by day and I thank God that he is always there for me.

I had come a long way since the hard days after Greg's disappearance, but I still had chosen not to speak to the media on sentencing day. This, however, didn't stop every paper running with the story anyway. I can't say I was surprised. I knew it was an incredible and unbelievable story, expecting it to be reported widely. No surprise, it was, and across the world. What I didn't expect was the misreporting, lazy journalism or maybe just plain nasty untruths that were being printed, mostly about me.

Greg had stood up in Crown Court and pleaded guilty to all the charges put against him. The Prosecuting Judge calling his treatment of me 'cruel and wicked'. His manipulation and crimes so clever and calculated that I never stood a chance.

As a victim there was a lifelong restraining order put in place, forbidding Greg from ever contacting myself or Karen to cause us any more pain.

So how was it, as the victim, that I was reading cruel untruths about myself and having to endure the most horrific outpouring of nastiness and victim shaming? How could this be fair? How could this be right?

Many media outlets had contacted me on sentencing day, all clamouring for an interview. I had steadfastly refused them all. We had had our justice; Greg was in prison and that was good enough for me. I didn't feel there was any more left to say. I had put a lid on the box marked 'James' and had kicked it well and truly away from me.

Perhaps foolishly I had believed there was no point in me giving an interview. Nothing at all to be gained from it. Greg Wilson had pleaded guilty to all the charges against him. Had been sentenced to six years in prison. Finally, the truth was out there. His lies exposed. Was there any need to rake over the coals now? Surely better to let the embers die down and let us all get back to some kind of normal.

5

Trolls Belong Under A Bridge

Any hope I had of continuing my journey of peace and healing were soon well and truly blown apart over the next few days.

These are just a few of the many thousands of comments posted online after sentencing day.

NonP.C.

There's no fool like an old fool.

Jd764

Greedy stupid old S L A G

Truth58

Oh dear! Another desperate woman gets duped – news? I don't think so.

Telmeso22

Should have her kids taken off her she's an absolute disgrace.

Misswigan88

Women love a man with money. Makes me sick.

Fatman45

This makes me laugh greedy old bag gets what she deserves

Kerryanna

She must be pretty thick!

Henry1415

Greedy and selfish. Looking for a WAG lifestyle! Thick woman.

BigTimD

Made my day another woman getting what she deserves

JuliaBenson

Gullible or what? Not sure she even deserves much sympathy.

Jules2468

Some women really need to use their brains well.

Had enough uk

Idiot woman blinded by alleged cash.

Runethelune

Her naivety knows no bounds.

SamoyedSam

No fool like a desperate old fool.

Masculinist

Females are so gullible – they will believe any rubbish a bloke tells them.

Complainer

Another dumb blonde.

AireborneVengance

Absolutely SERVES HER RIGHT! GREEDY SELFISH COW.

KensingtonPlace

Women are just desperate now a days.

Expat44

Gullible and greedy, "you cannot con an honest man."

Pilgrim_pete

Hahahahahahahahahahahahahaha Some women are so thick and stupid...

Howie D

Unbelievable, someone needs to hold her hands wherever she goes.

Catherine1978

Take me down to gullible city when you'll con me out of thousands if you're smooth and witty. What a silly billy she is.

Jk111

I'm sorry but you must be really thick to believe his stories.

I understand the anonymity of the internet can bring out the very worst in human nature. But in no way was I anticipating any of the vileness that was being spewed at me from every direction. It was overwhelming.

The press had fallen on the story like a pack of ravenous hyenas. Not bothering to take the time to check if the story they were running was true, or perhaps not caring, in their desperate haste to get it out there first.

I had met the fake 'James Scott' never imagining he had any money whatsoever. In fact I believed quite the opposite. I had always thought that I was the one who was more financially comfortable. Confident in the knowledge that, although not wealthy, he was a stand-up, run-of-the-mill good guy, working for the fire service, a great partner and a hands-on father to Charlie.

Any money in his family belonged to his successful mother, but he only made me aware of her 'success' after we had been in a relationship for 18 months. Prior to that I had believed she was a woman comfortably well off but nothing out of the ordinary.

Throughout our two-and-a-half-year relationship I had never given him a single penny or invested in any business whatsoever. I had not been ripped off by him as the papers so brazenly stated.

I had met his mother and stepfather in person, albeit briefly, as Greg had whisked me away on a fake emergency before we could engage in much conversation. I had also had, what I believed to be, relationships with all of his family. These relationships may have only been via phone calls, text messages and social media but I honestly believed I knew them well. On occasions I would speak to his sister on the phone and felt we were beginning to forge a close bond. I would hear his daughters in the background whilst they were speaking on the telephone with their 'father' and could hear them clearly ask him to say 'hi' to me.

I had met friends of his and acquaintances who all seemed to know him pretty well. Some of these people were 'real', believing him to be James Scott too and also part of his cruel deception. Whilst others we now know were fictitious, playing parts to heartlessly trick my family and friends and making Greg Wilson's alter ego, James Scott, appear totally credible.

The story circulating the world over, however, did not report the truth. Suggesting I had met a millionaire firefighter and that I was a money-hungry gold digger, cynical and shallow. Eventually giving him all my money in my desperate naivety, trying to hold onto him and his fortune.

A divorced, desperate single mother who, let's face it, was running out of any other options. Greedily lapping up every lie I was told. Choosing never to question anything, too blinded by the allure of cash to notice the countless red flags. But the fact was that none of it was true!

If I'm totally honest with myself, if I'd not known the actual truth and had been reading the story in the press like everyone else, the tale of another poor gullible woman, then I too would have had some misgivings. I would of course have felt some sympathy for her as a victim of a heartless, devious conman, but my sympathy would have had its limits. Thinking her somewhat foolish and naïve and that it was all just too good to be true. Wondering how she could have chosen to ignore so many red flags. Believing that it could never happen to me. Now I know different. Men like Greg Wilson can happen to anyone.

Reading vile comment after vile comment, I sobbed my heart out. I wanted to scream the truth at my open laptop. Tell these cruel people that they couldn't be more wrong about me and my family. Sick to the stomach with the injustice of it all. Greg Wilson had taken my family to hell and back, but we had stood strong and fought back. We regained the control, seen him put behind bars where he belonged. So how was this fair? Making me feel that I was the one living in what should be Greg's hell? That it had taken hold of me and was not letting go. Quickly dragging me down, making me the pitiful victim once more. Someone I had vowed never to be again.

We all know deep down that these cruel online bullies only deserve our disdain. I would have told anyone else that this was happening to, to ignore them, not give them the satisfaction of reading just one of their poisonous outpourings. When it happens to you though, it is completely different. I found myself unable to tear my eyes away. Reading comment after comment, desperate to find any shred of kindness and compassion from anyone. Now I know that this in itself is a form of self-harm, like picking at a scab, painful but impossible to stop.

My lovely husband even lost his patience with me at times. It was breaking his heart to see his wife so crushed by her cruel treatment at the hands of strangers. People I would never meet but who felt they had the right to judge and criticise me in the cruellest of ways.

These people didn't know us, didn't care, and would no doubt have already moved on to tearing their next victim down.

"Col, that's enough," Scott snapped at me, his brown eyes full of concern, gently taking the laptop out of my hands. "I can't stand by and watch you suffer like this all because of a bunch of arsehole bullies who wouldn't say boo to a goose in the real world."

This was one of the few times I have ever seen Scott angry, but I knew it was coming from a good place. It was hurting him to see me so upset and he was desperate for it to stop.

He kept hiding the laptop from me, but I would always manage to seek it out. My desperate need for validation and a crumb of compassion would continue. I would lock myself away in the bathroom for hours and scroll through website after website as tears ran down my face and fell in big drops onto the keyboard.

6

The Darkness And The Light

The days that followed were simply awful. For the first time I felt glad to be in lockdown. Having previously found the inability to see people lonely and isolating, now I was thankful for it. Glad to not have to see anyone. I was convinced that everyone would be talking about me, whispering and judging me, even laughing at me like the trolls had so cruelly done. It got to the point where I would not even go into my own garden, scared of any prying eyes that might be about, seeking me out to ridicule. Instead, I would lie on the sofa under the comforting weight of a blanket, hiding from the world, dark thoughts circulating constantly in my head. The despair was overwhelming me.

Poor Scott was left to deal with Charlie and his boys, to keep the normality of family life ticking over. We were relying too much on ready meals rather than home cooking. He was sick with worry for me but at a loss as to know how to make things better. How to get the old Coleen back. He could see I had retreated into my shell. Dark thoughts crept into my mind and took hold of me. If I'm truthful I just wanted to close my eyes sometimes, and never wake up. At times I contemplated making that happen. But thankfully my children's faces always dragged me back, keeping the bad thoughts at bay.

Karen didn't know what to do for the best. We were fifty miles apart from each other now, unable to meet up regularly like we always had. Unable to share a hug, a glass of wine or just to cry on each other's shoulders. But she was forever there for me, like she had always been, desperate to make me smile again. To see these online bullies for what they truly were and to rise above it all.

"They're a disgrace Col! We've not come all this way for a bunch of sad wankers, sitting in their grubby underpants in their mother's spare boxroom, to drag you down," she ranted. "They'd probably crap themselves if they ever actually came across a strong woman like you in real life."

Despite myself, I smiled. I loved my twin sister so much and knowing she was hurting from this, nearly as much as I was, although she was determined not to show it. How she wanted to take on all these bullies herself, tear a strip off them and set the record straight, warmed my heart.

"You know what you need to do?" she asked in a firm, no nonsense voice, "you need to get your side across. Let everyone know that all the stuff online is a load of rubbish, take the power back, not just sit at home feeling sorry for yourself. Pull your finger out and make things right."

Her words may have been true, but they still stung. I couldn't imagine doing anything that would draw more attention to myself. I had already had far too much of that, thank you very much. I was desperate to be back to my safe place, under my blanket on the sofa again. Alone with my thoughts. However, Karen hadn't finished, and I started to suspect some sort of family intervention had been discussed without my knowledge. And I feared fighting against it would prove to be futile.

Karen had spoken to Chris Bentham, the prosecuting Police officer in Greg's case, and between them they had taken things into their own hands. He had always been so supportive in our tireless three-year fight to get Greg to face justice. Always believing in us. He agreed with my sister that I needed to take the control back and get my side across. He was going to give a short interview about the case on the Radio 4 show *You and Yours* that day and wanted me to go on the following day to do the same.

I was completely horrified at the thought. I just couldn't, could I? My stomach lurched and all my instincts told me to say no and hide away again. The siren song of the sofa and my weighted blanket proving difficult to resist.

"You need to do this," Karen implored, her voice firm. "I promise it will help; I know you didn't want to speak to any of the tabloids, but this is different. It will be an interview and you'll get a chance to speak, to tell the story in your own words – get the truth out there. It's a consumer show that tackles all sorts of issues, not some tacky tabloid that just wants to get some provocative version out to boost their sales. They want the real story; they want their listeners to hear the truth." She paused before finishing with the words she knew would convince me to agree. "You could even help some people, make something good come from all the bad."

On and on, Karen reasoned with me. She can be a very determined woman, but more than that, I knew she was right. And the thought that there might be listeners who could actually be helped by our story, emboldened to take action themselves after being wronged, was the only convincing I really needed. I was incredibly nervous about being interviewed, but look what I had already been through and survived. What harm could this really do? And with an ember of hope sparking within me I eventually agreed.

Maybe this would help me too? I really hoped so, and anyway, could it really make things any worse after the way I had been feeling the last few days?

How glad I am now that I relented that gloomy dark afternoon, and my stubborn sister got her own way.

7

Getting My Voice Out There

Firstly, I spoke to Jon Douglas, a Reporter and Researcher from the BBC Radio 4 *You and Yours* show to give him more background on my story before the interview the following day with Winifred Robinson. Jon was kind and friendly, extremely easy to chat to. And once I started telling him my story the floodgates truly opened. Once opened, I couldn't stop, barely pausing to catch breath for well over an hour.

My whole life with Greg Wilson, aka 'James Scott', relayed to him in full chapter and verse. I don't think the poor man knew what had hit him, but he was clearly fascinated with the extreme lengths that Greg had gone to in his deception of so many innocent people. To keep his fake life and 'James Scott' alive.

"So, you really never gave him any money at all Coleen?" Jon questioned again, interrupting my heartfelt tale, obviously incredulous at the unfolding story. "This isn't the story I thought I would be hearing today, anything but. It's undoubtedly romance fraud alright, but nothing I've ever heard the like of before. I'm stunned and in truth it's something you would expect to see in a film."

"I know," I replied, "that's what is so upsetting. People are making all sorts of assumptions about me. They believe I met this man who I thought was loaded and this blinded me to all his lies, but the true story couldn't be further from that. My family and I have fought for years to get justice, to stop him hurting anyone else. So how is it fair that I'm the one being hurt all over again?"

After we had been talking for well over an hour, Jon wrapped up the call, confirming he would ring me again the following morning with details of the questions Winifred would most probably ask. The interview would be aired on Radio 4 on that morning's show. He reassured me not to worry as he knew I would do great. He told me the best thing I could do would be to get some rest and to definitely stay off the internet.

The interview the following morning went well. I was incredibly nervous but tried my hardest to keep the shakiness out of my voice. It wasn't easy but I knew I had to get the true story out there. Winifred was lovely and clearly knew how to put me at ease. I felt like I was talking to a friend rather than an interviewer. She asked a few questions – how had I met 'James Scott'? About his deceit, his devious manipulation. How he lived as a member of our family for two and a half years, completely loved and trusted until his lies eventually started to catch up with him. The interview that aired later that morning was maybe eight minutes long and, in that time, barely touched on the extremes of Greg's behaviour. But it was true, what had actually happened. No media lies, no spin, no twisted words cleverly retold to serve me up on a platter to the hungry trolls. We've all seen it happen time and time again to celebrities, the unflattering photo with an accompanying headline stating how glamorous or slim the person looks. Literally lighting the touchpaper and standing well back waiting for the flames of fury and indignation to rage.

It's awful to see any human being treated that way. But if I'm honest, when it comes to celebrities, we all think to ourselves on some level they made a choice to be in the limelight, knew what they were signing up for, getting themselves into. I really never envisaged for one minute that victims of crime, any Joe Bloggs on the street, was fair game too. I know better now.

I felt more positive just taking that one step. That one short interview had empowered me a little. I had started to stand up for myself. It felt good. Baby steps maybe, but steps in the right direction, nevertheless.

My family and friends were all lovely, saying that I had spoken well on air and that they were extremely proud. I even received a few messages from strangers on my social media accounts, kind words, supportive words that had been in short supply to date. These words made me smile, restored my faith in humanity once again.

Jon also rang that afternoon. Seeing his name flash up on my screen, I assumed it was a courtesy call, a 'good luck in the future' follow up type of thing. And that was indeed what he was calling for, but also for so much more.

"Hi Coleen." Jon greeted me with a cheery tone to his voice. "Well done on the interview, you did really good, came over incredibly well."

It was a relief to hear his words. I knew in my heart the interview had gone well but to get Jon's confirmation on it was validation to me.

"Thank you, Jon, I'm so glad I did it. It's already made me feel so much better, much stronger." I laughed in a self-deprecating manner, "although I hated how my voice sounded on the radio, am I really that northern and squeaky?"

He chuckled at this and reassured me. "Absolutely everyone hates the sound of their own voice, even actors and politicians who have been interviewed hundreds of times. In all honestly you sounded great." He paused for a second before continuing. "That isn't the only reason I've called you though. Your story really is amazing. Nearly unbelievable, but all true. I can still barely get my head around it."

I agreed with him. "It's definitely not the 'what attracted the dumb blonde to the millionaire firefighter and give him all her cash' story that's doing the rounds, that's for sure."

"Exactly," Jon exclaimed, enthusiastically. "It's a jaw drop-ping story that needs to be shared. It would make a fantastic documentary or podcast series. Get the story out there and explore it in much more depth. The psychology of 'James', why Greg did it? His reasons, his motivations, what his early life was like. People need to hear this and hopefully it could go on to help others. I know that that is yours and your family's driving force. To make sure he can't do this again to another family."

He went on to explain that making this a reality would be both difficult and time consuming. The country was still currently in lockdown and with him having a full-time job with the BBC we would need to work on this solely in his spare time. He was still adamant he wanted to do it. Felt that this was too good a story not to be pursued.

"What I need you to do, Coleen, is to think back, put yourself back into your life six years ago, back to 2014. I know it will be harrowing but I've got faith in you. Make a thorough timeline of your life, your feelings, everything you can remember. I understand that it will be tough, but it will be worth it. Speak to your family, work with your sister and let's get your story heard."

I knew he was right. It was time to take back the control and focus on the good. So, I agreed with Jon and thanked him for all his kind words.

Once the call had ended, without hesitation, I phoned my twin.

"Kazza, how do you feel about getting the true 'James Scott' story out there?" My words tumbled out as soon as I heard her voice on the other end of the line. "Let everyone know the truth of it all, every detail, stand up for ourselves. To no longer be the victims."

Karen was completely in agreement. "Anything that gets the truth out there about that poisonous little git sounds like a no brainer to me."

My sister was never one for mincing her words.

And that afternoon, once that decision was made, we never anticipated this would be the start of a three-year journey culminating in a number 1 rated BBC Sounds podcast, a book and filming documentaries.

8

A Step Back

I sat in silence, chewing absentmindedly on the end of my pen as I stared at the blank sheet of paper laid out on the table in front of me. The only sounds were the wall clock ticking the seconds away and the distant spin of the washing machine in the kitchen down the hall. The faithful appliance completing yet another load of Charlie and my stepsons' dirty clothes. Football strips and socks. Caring for three young boys meant there was a never-ending stream of dirty socks to be dealt with. The washing, the sorting into pairs and then putting away in drawers, it was a cycle that never ceased. However, dealing with a mountain of laundry seemed a doddle compared with putting my feelings and thoughts down on paper. The blank page felt like it was mocking me. Telling me to give up before I had even started. I wasn't a writer after all, neither was I a Journalist like Jon. I just didn't have a clue where to start yet and there was so much I wanted to say.

I picked up my cup of coffee. It was stone cold, but I took a large sip anyway. I distinctly heard the sound of someone clearing their throat. It jolted me back into the here and now, remembering that my sister was also with me. Not in person of course, as we were in lockdown, but on a Zoom call via my laptop. The expression on her face was clearly displaying the fact that she was getting a little impatient at my reluctance to begin. She was as keen as mustard to get things started.

"Come on Coleen, let's get this going. I hope you've got plenty more paper than that one sheet. This is going to take a while." I saw she too was holding a large mug, clearly needing some caffeine to get this task started.

"I know, I know." I answered staring at my pink painted nails that were already chipped and bitten. I had felt the need to put a little makeup on and do my nails. Silly really but I knew if I had my warpaint on and felt I looked good I would feel more confident in myself. More like the old me. Conversely, I could see that Karen, sipping away at her mug of coffee, was fresh faced. She had her hair scraped back into a messy bun, a small tea stain visible on her old, frayed pyjama top. She was happy to wear her lockdown uniform to get this job done. She felt no need to wear armour to give her confidence. My sister was champing at the bit to write our story down, get our truth out there. But even she realised there was so much to it. Would we really include everything? Would it all be too much?

Greg Wilson was still biologically Charlie's father. Neither one of us could give a flying toss about him but as a family we all still wanted to protect Charlie. Greg would always be his biological father.

Karen's words echoed in my ears. "We need to tell the whole story, but we also need to protect Charlie. Once it's all out there it's there forever. There's no going back." She let out a gusty sigh. "I think we should write it all down to start with, warts and all, and then in time we can decide what we include and what we don't. But first things first we should get down absolutely everything that odious little shit ever said and did."

I couldn't help agreeing with her. At least if we did a thorough timeline, wrote down everything we could, then in time we could decide how much of it ever saw the light of day. But at least we would have the full unabridged version.

We all, as a family, loved Charlie and we were going to protect him, no matter what. But he would also need to know all the facts in time. He deserved to know everything about his biological father. It was his right.

At present Charlie was still too young to know much, but I did try to be honest with him wherever possible. I'd tell him whatever was age appropriate for him to hear. Scott was going to adopt him, make him his 'forever dad', as Charlie called him, and if there was any justice in the world, surely no one would try to stop that? Once Charlie was adopted Greg Wilson would fail to have any power over us. He would lose the little bit of control he still had left.

Charlie realised that he had had another dad, one who had not been very nice to some people and who no longer saw us. That was how he described it, the innocent description from a young child. He was a really contented little boy. This made us happy. He was now living in a safe, secure, love-filled family home.

I nodded my head with conviction and smiled at Karen on the screen. "You're right, I know you are. OK, we'd all best buckle up because this is going to be one hell of a bumpy ride."

We talked for hours on that first day, taking us right back to September 2014 and the first time I met the fictitious 'James Scott'. Our coffee date, his comical taste in clothing, and right through our lives together until he finally fled from the home we shared together, in February 2017, leaving me heartbroken. I wrote until my hand was numb and my pen ran dry, recalling everything right up until his sentencing only a couple of days prior on 8th April 2020.

I cried many tears, as did Karen, but to be honest there was also laughter and lots of it. We laughed so much the tears ran down our faces. His ridiculous hats, him shaving every single hair from his body until he resembled a pasty plucked chicken, saying it was necessary, so his skin didn't chafe in the heat when wearing his firefighting gear. His high-pitched girly giggle. We could even find humour in some of the lies we had been told, the sheer audacity of the man. Now with the luxury of hindsight we really could see how unhinged it all was. I almost wished he had been proven mentally ill, at least it would have been easier to understand some of his actions. Maybe even forgive to a certain degree. Standing up in Court, Greg's Barrister had used mental illness as a defence, claiming it wasn't all Greg's fault. He couldn't be held truly accountable for his actions. But Judge Adkins wasn't having any of it. Greg Wilson, and Greg Wilson alone, was guilty. He knew exactly what he was doing every step of the way. He was not ill, just a very cruel and callous man and we had been unlucky to become his victims.

He deserved every year of the six-year sentence he received. In fact, he was lucky as he could, and in many people's eyes should, have faced a much stricter punishment. He had been guilty of a much more serious crime than the ones he was incarcerated for.

9

One Fight Too Many

I knew that Karen and I were going to have to take a lengthy walk down memory lane. Piecing together so many recollections of our time with Greg so that we could produce a thorough timeline to give to Jon. It wasn't going to be easy, we knew that, but we really wanted to do it.

However, there was one part of our story that hung heavily in the air between us. Karen and I rarely quarrelled but one particular issue had caused a disagreement to bubble over into an argument between us. Not a rift exactly, but at that time, years ago, a couple of days had passed without us speaking to one another. Us not speaking on a daily basis was unthinkable. This was the only time Greg had ever come between us. The issue we hadn't agreed on was what criminal charges should be put to him.

There were, of course, the many charges of fraud and deception. However, there was also another crime he was guilty of, one which the Crown Prosecution Service were actively pushing for him to be charged with – the crime of statutory rape. The CPS claimed that as I had been duped into restarting a sexual relationship with Greg, he was indeed guilty of rape. It was a sexual assault committed against me. I had believed there was absolutely no chance of falling pregnant again. He'd had a vasectomy after all, and shown me the medical report with a zero sperm count.

Greg knew how terribly fearful I was of becoming pregnant again. We'd been careful before, but it had still happened. It had been a hard decision to terminate that pregnancy, and I had been so sad. But we made the decision together. It caused me such grief and regret, although I knew at the time it was the right thing to do, I could not ever contemplate going through that again.

Knowing this he still chose to fake that medical report, shaved his pubic area, applied fake bruising to his genitals. Why go to such extraordinary lengths? All just to get his leg over again? Greg had played God with my very life. Dreadfully deceiving me. And when inevitably I had fallen pregnant again, he had professed it was a miracle. He told me that aborting the previous pregnancy had been a dreadful mistake and this was the child coming back. Giving us a second chance to do the right thing. This was how it was meant to be. The man was sick and twisted to his very core.

It was coercion, the CPS had stated, manipulating me into a sexual relationship that I would never ever have engaged in had I known the risk. This case was unique, but they were adamant that this should be addressed. To set a precedent for the future.

The CPS do not push for charges to be made unless they are extremely confident of a conviction. As with most things in life, sadly it all comes down to money. Unless they are pretty certain that the person will be found guilty, they won't push ahead with a case. I could be forging a path for other victims in the future.

I knew all of this but, try as I might, I could not agree to Greg being charged with this crime. It just didn't sit well with me. Rape is such a vile crime, and I didn't want me or my innocent son Charlie's name connected with it. Documented in the press, forever tarnished by it. The story living on through the internet, forever.

I questioned how the CPS classed my case as statutory rape. I had consented, I had been in love with Greg. How was there even a crime at all? The CPS strongly disagreed. It was criminality, I had been lied to and manipulated. They compared it to someone knowingly having HIV who didn't inform prospective partners. Would they still have consented? Of course not. That was recognised in the courtroom as statutory rape so my experience would be too.

Chris Bentham understood my reservations and concerns and encouraged me to do what was right for me. What I felt I could live with.

"Don't worry Coleen I believe we have enough evidence to get a good verdict against him despite this, but it really is your decision to make."

I decided no, it was just too much more for me to face. My entire sex life being pulled apart on the stand, scrutinised in minute detail. I wanted justice all right, but I wanted my mental health to be intact too. Truthfully, I hated Greg but didn't want 'rapist' added to his catalogue of crimes. Mindful of his other children, I didn't want this blighting their lives too.

Although Karen didn't initially agree with my decision, she understood why I had made it. She had tried to talk me round a bit, hence our little spat. She told me that if he were found guilty of this crime too his sentence would be longer, and would keep him away from hurting others. But when she realised I was adamant she let the matter drop. She understood my mind was made up. Karen is, and always has been, my greatest supporter. Although I was technically older, by 20 minutes, it often felt like she was the mature, more protective sibling, always looking out for me. We hadn't let Greg destroy our family before, so we certainly weren't going to allow him to do it now.

So, my mind was made up. Greg would not be charged with that crime. The CPS and my Barrister were disappointed, but it was my decision to make. And I knew for myself and my family I had made the right one.

10

Playing The Part

We were working hard constructing the timeline for Jon. Having gone way back to the beginning we detailed as much as we could. I did the majority of the talking whilst Karen wrote down page after page of our recollections on her tatty old notebook with a blue biro. Both of us had to stop at times, just to shake our heads at the audacity of the man, barely believing it ourselves even though we had lived through it all. We still found his lies so shocking.

My life was changed forever when I first met Greg back in that Durham Starbucks coffee shop on an unseasonably warm day in September of 2014.

As we had chatted over coffee, he had proudly told me he was a firefighter, part of White Watch working out of Darlington fire station. He was so compelling when he talked about his love for his job, incredibly knowledgeable and so passionate. This knowledge we now know was acquired from his late father who had in fact been the firefighter in the family. The only one.

Greg wasn't one just for talking though. Oh no, he liked to back his stories up with props. Leave no one in any doubt that his persona of 'James Scott – hero firefighter' was true. He would often wear his full firefighter's uniform, looking totally authentic and smelling strongly of smoke. The outfit, we discovered in time, he had bought from an ex-firefighter. A little something off eBay bought to spice up the bedroom antics for Greg and his wife Rachel.

The emails and many text messages I would receive from Durham and Darlington fire service looked so real. He also showed me many photos of his colleagues and messages he had received from them. He was so popular at his workplace. His friends and family would also message me. My family and I would hear the many telephone conversations he would have with his colleagues and friends, discussing shifts or just having a chat and arranging to go for a pint. Conversations where we could clearly hear someone else on the other end of the line.

I received gifts and kind words from his workmates, people I now know never existed. Greg really was so thorough in his attention to detail. It sickens me to say but, on some level, you have to marvel at his cunning. It takes guts to do what he did. I can't even tell a fib when a girlfriend asks me if her outfit makes her bum look big, but the magnitude of lies that he could tell, and how he could remember them all, shows an intelligence that is hard to fathom. If only he had used these skills for good, he could have made such a positive change in the world.

Even before his career as 'James Scott – hero firefighter' he had another backstory that was similarly heroic. He had constructed a career for before the time he had met me, and it also came into play. Before the fire service there had been 'James Scott – hero paramedic'. He had worked in this field for a few years before going into the fire service. He said he would always have become a firefighter, to take after his dad. It was a calling to him.

Of course, he had never been a paramedic either, but he had clearly done his research to back up this lie too, as once again his knowledge in the field was staggering. As far as I am aware he had no links whatsoever to this career but his attention to detail when describing the profession was impressive.

I suspect he took all his lies seriously, researched them fully like a method actor absorbing themselves into their role. Reading medical journals, binge-watching medical shows and hospital dramas. Who knows, maybe he even hung around hospitals in his spare time, getting a feel for it. I sincerely hope not. That thought makes me shudder, picturing him walking down hospital corridors like it was his second home.

No one ever doubted him though. And it really does go to show, if you speak with confidence and conviction on almost anything, people will tend to believe you. Most people are honest and trustworthy, and they regard others in the same way.

I always think with Greg it was like the tale of the *emperor's new clothes*. Nobody wanted to point a finger at him and call him a liar as the crowd all hung off his every word.

Karen paused for a second from her frantic note taking. "Do you remember his driving though Col? That was really insane. He drove so fast, so recklessly, but we all believed he was safe and capable as he had his advanced driving qualification."

I didn't need to look at my sister's face, prominent on my laptop screen, to know she was rolling her eyes. "I mean come on, it's amazing the jumped-up little dick didn't kill us all. It was like being in the passenger seat with Lewis Hamilton."

She was right again. Being a passenger when Greg was driving was akin to being on a white-knuckle rollercoaster ride. Time and time again he reassured us he had passed his advanced driving test for when he drove the ambulances, so we felt safe, that he knew what he was doing. He was so convincing. Now we know he had never been on any advanced driving courses. He was just incredibly dangerous and a demented thrill-seeker.

"Not just the driving though, he took things further than that Karen."

I told my sister about an occasion when Greg and I had been on a date. Not long into our relationship. We went for a Sunday afternoon drive, keen to discover a nice country pub to pop into for a spot of lunch. Just me and him in the car going for a nice long drive. To my horror there had been an accident further on up the country lane ahead.

"Stay in the car, Princess," he had instructed firmly, as he flung the car door open and went bounding out, striding over to the scene of the accident with an air of authority and purpose.

It was 'James to the rescue'. He made sure that an ambulance had been called and barked instructions to the few bystanders. They had all quickly fallen into line and done exactly what he had told them, just relieved that an obviously medically trained safe pair of hands had arrived. Not for a second doubting his authority or integrity. Not considering for a second that the words he spoke, and his actions, were probably copied straight from an episode of *Casualty*.

Karen's voice was aghast. "He really had to inveigle his way into everything, didn't he? He needed to feel he was the man of the hour, saving the world. It's sickening, it really is."

"Did I ever tell you the time we went down south for a long weekend with Laura and Katie?" I asked my sister, not sure if she already knew the story. "It was just after Charlie was born. The time we went ice skating?"

Karen was quiet for a moment, thinking back. "Yes, you did." She let out a little laugh. "Didn't he play 'Doctor James in the house' again then?"

I couldn't help but smile at Karen's description. It was spot on. My sister was never backward at coming forward in her disdain for Greg and his lies.

We had gone away for a few days to London with my girls and had decided to go ice skating. It would be a fun family activity and a bit of exercise too. Charlie was still so little that I stayed back in the viewing gallery, nice and warm and with a mug of hot chocolate and big slice of cake. I had an excellent view of the rink though, and was enjoying watching Greg and the girls have fun on the ice.

The fun didn't last long though, as a middle-aged man took a nasty-looking tumble and landed in a messy heap on the ice. Even from where I was seated, I could clearly see the blood rapidly staining the ice red. My heart was in my mouth as I helplessly watched on. But I shouldn't have feared, there was Greg again, kneeling down helping the injured man, ushering everyone back. He was in control. I felt so proud of my man that day, as did my girls. They had rushed over to me afterwards, gushing about how he had helped the injured man and was a real hero. Greg had smiled modestly. Hero was a role he loved to play.

A member of staff from the ice rink had even come over afterwards to thank him and shake his hand. Telling him how glad he was that a medic had been there to help.

He had even had occasion to help me. His medical 'knowledge' came into play in my life also. This, in my opinion, was the most sinister time. I was supposedly the love of his life. The mother to his baby son, but still, that didn't stop him. The need to play the hero was just too strong. Charlie's birth had been extremely traumatic and along with me being 42 years old, and having been on bedrest for months, the doctor confirmed I would need injections of blood thinners to keep me healthy. They were fearful about the possibility of blood clots. These injections could be administered at home, by a district nurse, or at my GP surgery by a qualified medic. James had eagerly stepped forward to offer his expertise – he was a qualified medic, after all. He was never doubted for a second and was given all the paraphernalia to inject me at home.

He had jabbed me twice a day for over a month. It was not pleasant, but he would just brush off my discomfort and the fact that I was covered in horrendous bruises. He claimed it was just due to my anaemia. In time the bruises faded but now I'm left with knowledge that isn't so quick to fade away. The troubling realisation that I had been very lucky indeed. Quite clearly, he was completely clueless at administering the injections but, nevertheless, had injected me daily for that month. I was lucky bruises and mild discomfort were the only things I suffered with. I could so easily have encountered something far more sinister, like a life-threatening air bubble.

This wouldn't have even entered his head. The roles he needed to play were always going to be far more important than my safety.

We were all just unwitting actors forced into his game of twisted reality. His desire to take centre stage always the driving force behind him.

11

Thinking On His Feet

Greg had introduced me to some fake friends along the way, people on his payroll. He had genuine friends too who we mutually knew, people he met since our relationship started. They were victims of his lies, just like us. However, I don't think he ever feared meeting someone in the real world, someone who knew the real him. Someone that could blow his lies completely apart and bring them all out into the open. I now know that this did happen on one occasion. Only once in nearly three years of lies.

During our relationship he would take me to places he so easily could have bumped into someone from his 'real life'. Restaurants he took his wife Rachel to, places in the city of Sunderland where her family still lived, where he had been raised. But we never met anyone he knew. On all of these occasions there had never been a friendly nod, a tap on the shoulder or shout from across the street from a friend who recognised him. He really did have the luck of the Devil. Did he get a thrill from this? Some sort of adrenaline rush from always hiding in plain sight? I really think he did. The stakes were high but he loved the thrill, knowing at any minute he could be discovered. But he believed he was invincible.

It was, however, on a family day out many miles from home, a visit to Staffordshire, where his lies could have been so easily uncovered. His web of deceit torn down. The truth discovered.

Charlie was only a few months old at this time so had been left with Grandma Jennifer for the day. Mum was happy, she loved nothing better than an afternoon of cuddles and cartoons. We had set off bright and early to Alton Towers – a theme park full of adventure and white-knuckle rides. It was a beautiful spring morning and, with Laura and her then boyfriend in tow, we were looking forward to a fun filled day. She had been nagging for ages to go to Alton Towers as it had been many years since we had last been as a family. Katie, not so keen, had already made plans when he announced we were going and that the tickets were all sorted and paid for. Laura was so excited, jumping up and down on the spot and reaching in to give Greg a huge hug. Thanking him for his thoughtfulness. He had beamed from ear to ear, playing the part of the generous, loving stepfather once again.

Greg had pulled me into the hug at that point. "You're very welcome, Laura. Nothing's too much trouble to keep my girls happy. We'll have a smashing day, I'll see to that."

Admittedly, roller coasters and long queues were not my first choice for a nice day out but it didn't matter. It was a small sacrifice to see Laura so happy.

So, with the four of us packed into Greg's car with enough sandwiches, pop and crisps to keep us going for a good few hours, we set off on our way. Greg was singing along to his playlist, making everyone laugh as he imitated each singer in turn. He really did have a knack for playing the part of someone else. And as always, he loved to have all eyes on him.

We had been at the park for a few hours, enjoyed a couple of white-knuckle rides and were eating bags of bright pink sticky candyfloss when we heard a man's voice behind us.

"All right Wilson, buddy? Long time no see, how's it going matey?"

We all turned around to see who and where this voice had come from. A pleasant looking, stocky man in his late thirties was smiling at Greg. He was beckoning him over with his hand. His other arm was down by his side, and we could all clearly see he was an amputee, his right arm stopping at the elbow joint.

Honestly, I can't remember Greg appearing even slightly uneasy or flustered by the man's sudden appearance. He just sauntered casually over to him and enthusiastically returned his greeting. He introduced the man to us all, telling us he was a friend from his early days. Greg later told me that they had been in the fire service together many years before. The man, like us, was out for a family day with his wife and young son. We all warmly exchanged greetings and Greg slung his arm around the man's shoulders and steered him slightly away from the group so they could talk more privately. His wife fussed with their young son who was getting impatient and grizzly at not being on the next ride.

Laura turned to me, her face was mirroring the puzzled expression that no doubt was all over mine too.

"Why has he just called James, Wilson?" she questioned. "That's a bit odd."

I nodded in agreement. I had been thinking the exact same thing. "God knows. I'm as confused as you are love."

Less than a minute later and Greg was back beside us, his friend now having wandered off towards the next attraction with his family. He had a massive grin spread on his face and was fizzing with excitement.

"What's the chances of me bumping into my old mucker Jonesy?" he exclaimed, shaking his head as if not quite believing it himself. "I've not seen that fella in years, and he's barely changed a bit. A bloody legend in the fire service, he is."

"But who is he?" I interrupted with confusion. "You say he was in the fire service with you but why did he call you Wilson? Who's Wilson?"

Greg threw his head back and roared with laughter. "Wilson is me Col." He took my hand and planted a kiss on the back of it. "Wilson was my nickname you see, when I started my fire service training all those years ago. All the guys had a nickname. When you're that close to people, rely on them with your life, they become like family to you."

His eyes had misted over a little as he reminisced about those early days. Days we now know never even existed.

"But why Wilson?" I was still confused. "I get nicknames, but your name is James Scott."

He rolled his eyes as if I were being purposefully dim. "He wasn't calling **me** Wilson." He started pulling on my hand to move me over to the next ride, hurrying me along and waving at Laura and her boyfriend to follow us. "He was calling me 'Will'. The 'son' is just a term of endearment as I was always the young one of the group."

He went further to explain how the nickname 'Will' had come about as one day they had needed someone to undertake some sort of exercise and space was restricted. Greg had quickly jumped forward to volunteer as he was one of the smallest and slightest trainees, but without a doubt one of the most tenacious. Always happy to put himself forward. And of course he had got the job done, much to the admiration of the rest of the guys. And therefore, earning himself the nickname 'Will' from then on. As in 'Where there's a will there's a way'.

He was the one in the group who wouldn't let any obstacle get in his way. Would always find a way of making things happen. He went on to tell us the many nicknames the guys he trained with all had. Some of them were hilarious and with such funny backstories. I was soon in fits of laughter with his tales and anecdotes. It put me in mind of the television programme *London's Burning* which I had always watched as a child, with my dad. They all had funny nicknames too. It made perfect sense.

Whether he had this story already in his arsenal for a situation just like this, or had just come up with it on the spot, I will never know. What I do know is that we never doubted the truth of it. He had never broken character for a single second, never got flustered or panicked. His story was seamless. We all believed him. Why wouldn't we?

Now years later we know that guy wasn't a firefighter. Didn't lose his arm in a nasty accident at a house fire. He was stationed with Greg Wilson in the Army in Germany and most probably lost his limb serving his country. 'Wilson' is what he had shouted that day. It was Greg's name after all and how he knew him. There never was a 'Will'. Just a 'James Scott', a very devious, calculating liar, who was smiling inside at just how clever he was. Free once more to deceive another day.

12

The Role He Was Born To Play

Karen and I left nothing out. We thought back over everything; the harrowing, the amusing, the just plain ridiculous, and the timeline grew from there. We detailed everything up to the present day. Our first dates, the pregnancies, his health scares, his family traumas and him deserting me on what should have been the happiest day of my life – our wedding day. Me left behind, broken-hearted and reeling from the shock of it all, our son barely a year old. The timeline started on his first contact with me on the dating app, and proceeded to cover everything to date.

There was one particular lie he told that hurt me deeply. It was at one of his plea hearings. He stated that I was the guilty one, not him. I was the one who decided to swindle my own twin sister. I was the one that concocted the whole story and forced him into playing along because he was so under my spell. It was ludicrous, and everyone knew it, but it still hurt.

There was no doubt about it, he was a clever man but unashamedly conniving and calculating too. Committing audacious crimes that impacted widely and cost his victims dearly. But also, we discovered that he was a small-time grubby thief too. The petty crimes he committed out of sheer greed, emptying Charlie's money box, stealing from other children. The Christmas that I was on bedrest when I was heavily pregnant, he had kindly offered to post Christmas cards for family and friends. Each envelope contained cash. Christmas gifts were out of the question that year because I was not up to shopping. These cards, I now know, never reached any of their destinations. The contents intended for family and friend's children ended up in his own pocket. At the time I couldn't understand why I had not been thanked for the cash gifts, thinking people rude and ungrateful. Now I know they had nothing to thank me for because they had never received the cash or the Christmas card. They must have been so disappointed in me at the time.

I even have reason to believe, now knowing the workings of the man, that he took my medication and tried to sell it on. I had been prescribed painkillers to take after the termination. I never took these painkillers; I hadn't found the pain too bad and didn't want to be zonked out. However, weeks later I couldn't understand why this medication was no longer in the bathroom cabinet where I had stored it. He had informed me he had returned the tablets to the pharmacy, not wanting me to see them and be reminded of what I had been through. I thought at the time this was a nice gesture, but not necessary. It was not until much later, after he had absconded, that I was told from one of Laura's friends that Greg had approached him and asked if he knew anyone who would buy the tablets. Laura's friend had been shocked but hadn't told her or me, as didn't want to cause trouble. However, my tablets were gone, and I find it hard to believe that he actually ever did return them to the NHS. More likely he found someone else to pass them on to, for a price of course.

Affable Greg also had many contacts, or so he made us believe. He always knew how to get a good deal for someone. Whether it be concert or festival tickets or on sporting events. Laura and some of her friends had given him money to secure Leeds tickets for the Autumn weekend festival in 2017. They all received confirmation emails which contained contact numbers, reference booking codes – they certainly appeared legitimate. But again, in time, we realised this too was a scam. Money defrauded from innocent 17-year-olds who had to work Saturday jobs to scrimp and save the money to pay for their ticket. When his fraud came to light, he had already been gone from our lives for months. It sickened my entire family and again, we came together to pool our limited resources so that the girls weren't left out of pocket. It was the right thing for us to do.

In some ways these crimes are some of his worst. A true indication of the levels he was quite happy to sink to. These crimes obviously not as newsworthy as others, and not included in his catalogue of offences. But to us, still unforgivable.

I read back over the timeline and felt an element of shock myself, at what had been my life. The first six months or so, back in 2014, just showed a blossoming, happy romance between me and Greg. He was always so attentive and loving, easily fitting into my family unit as if it were just meant to be. A rock to our family, someone to rely on, always there in a crisis.

Our first hurdle, documented in the timeline, was of course our unexpected pregnancy. We had been careful, taking precautions, but at 41 years of age I had discovered I was pregnant. Together we had decided on a termination. Greg was very supportive, and I decided, as is every woman's right, that it was the best decision to make. However, it lay heavily on me. And even though I knew it was the right decision, it was not something I could ever contemplate doing again. He selflessly went for a vasectomy. Our families were complete, he said, so it made perfect sense. Now we know this too was lies. No procedure took place. The phone calls, appointments, medical reports, even the bruising on his genitals, all fabricated. And because of these lies and deception, I fell pregnant again.

At this point in reading the timeline, I began to cry. Great big, snotty tears. I still find it so difficult to understand why he did these things. I doubt I'll ever understand. Lying about having a vasectomy is the one thing I'll never comprehend. When the Police first told me their suspicions that he had never had the procedure and they had discovered that there was no Doctor Maddison, no appointments ever booked at the Woodlands Clinic in Darlington, I was heartbroken. These were cruel, life changing lies. Lies that plunged me into a living nightmare. Who does something like that? And even more importantly, why the hell would they?

To this day this, in my opinion, is the worst crime. The worst deception, immoral and unforgivable. And has been one of the hardest to rectify, because in the eyes of the law, little Charlie didn't even exist. A fake father on his birth certificate actually meant that my son also had a fake name. A name, I was scared, would possibly blight his future forever.

"Do I need to put all this down in writing? Go through it all again?" I asked of Karen. "It's all out there in the press, in the court reports, for everyone to read. I hate to even have to think about it again, all the pain that man caused."

Karen cajoled me gently; she understood my reticence but knew it was something I needed to do.

"Come on Col, look how far we've all come. If we're going to do this, we're going to do it right. The whole bloody thing, every sorry tale and evil thing he did, we get it down in black and white."

Karen's was the one voice I had to listen to. Greg Wilson had cost her so dearly too. Defrauded her from her life savings, she had lost her home, her properties, was forced into bankruptcy, sent into a spiral of despair. Her life was also changed forever.

13

Cheap-Arse Friday

G reg had received a long prison sentence – six years in total, for his crimes. Most of the criminal charges he faced were for his financial frauds. These misdemeanours were far reaching and elaborate in nature. He had cleverly constructed them with such meticulous details, going to great lengths to convince everyone of their authenticity. He had cunningly weaved a web of so many lies, intertwining real, completely innocent people with fake ones, real documents with forgeries so that even the Police and judicial system were staggered by the lengths he had gone to.

Karen had been badly burnt by Greg. She was far from the only one, but unlike the Northeast businesses and charities that he defrauded, she had not just lost a lot she had in fact lost everything. She had entrusted the entirety of her life savings to him, trusting him as her soon-to-be brother-in-law, confident the decision to do so was right for her and her family. Hearing and seeing so much evidence to back up the fact that her investments were sound.

She had been confident that her money was safe, and she

would reap the rewards in time. This was not to be the case. And , if there were so many well-respected businessmen and women duped by him, realistically what chance did she really ever have?

When the heat had become too much for Greg and he knew his deception had been discovered, that he could no longer spin more tales, keep the lies going, it was time for him to flee. Karen was hit with the devastating blow, full force. She was penniless. Greg had cost her and me our careers. But Karen had lost so much more than that – the rental properties she owned with her ex-husband, her own home – everything. But much worse than that, she had lost her sense of who she was in the world, what her purpose was. She had lost it all. She fought hard to claw her way back, but the damage was just too severe. She had to face the truth; she had no choice but to file for bankruptcy.

"It still hurts now to think about it, even though plenty of time has passed since then," she admitted, her voice low and thoughtful as she absent-mindedly chewed on the end of her pen and shuffled the papers of our growing timeline. "43 years old and having worked hard my entire life to end up with nothing." Karen dropped her pen suddenly and dabbed at her eyes with the edge of her pyjama sleeve. She was clearly upset having to remember the hardships of that time and get it all detailed down in the timeline. The scrimping and doing without, having to borrow to make ends meet. The difficulty of just getting through one day to the next. Knowing in the back of her mind that the person who had caused all this pain was out there at that time. He would no doubt be flashing the cash, her cash, living his best life. His struggling victims long-forgotten as he moved on to his next ones.

I could see her clearly on my laptop screen shaking her head as if trying to force herself out of her distressing memories. She gave a little melancholy laugh. "Do you remember 'cheap-arse Friday'?"

Of course, I remembered. It was about the only thing I had to look forward to back then. It hadn't been much, but we had at least had something. I smiled fondly at my sister's image on the screen.

"Cheap-arse Friday? How could I forget? Those evenings were the only bit of fun we had in those days."

Money was in very short supply then, but Ryan had insisted once a week we should all have a night off and go out for a few hours. Forget our troubles for at least that evening, try to feel normal again, more like the people we used to be.

Charlie was still so clingy, suffering badly with separation anxiety. He was at his happiest with only certain people, me, Mum and his Godmother Yvonne. Charlie adored his grandma and Yvonne and loved to be with them. They were the only other people apart from me and his sisters he would settle with.

Ryan had spoken to Yvonne, and she was delighted to offer her babysitting services every Friday night. She thought it was a great idea. She was so proud of the family that we hadn't let Greg cause a rift between us and we had pulled even closer together. So 'cheap-arse Friday' was well and truly born.

It wasn't anything grand, just a few alcoholic drinks and savoury snacks at Karen and Ryan's house. There would be crisps, nuts and mini chipolatas, which we would joke looked like Greg's tiny todger. Admittedly it was childish but made us laugh all the same. This, all followed by a cheap bottle of wine at the Lambton Arms pub in Chester-Le-Street. They often had a live band playing on a Friday night, free of charge, which made the evening go with a swing. Okay, it was a far cry from the Michelin starred restaurants and extravagant hotel stays that Greg would take me to, but honestly much more my style. Those Fridays were so important for all of us. They got us out of our homes and collectively helped us to heal. They might have been hard days back then, but we still managed to have a laugh. That's the thing with life – if you look hard enough, there's always some good to be found. Sometimes it's difficult to do but it's always worth making the effort.

The modern marvel that is social media meant we always knew, on some level, what Greg was up to. No doubt we were long-forgotten by him, but he was still, sometimes more than necessary, the main topic of conversation in our family. Our need to see justice done was a flame that burned within us all. Friends would get in touch if someone had seen him out and about, or thought they had. Never mind 'Where's Wally' it was 'Where's Walter Mitty' in our lives. My girls were like the FBI when it came to keeping tabs on their erstwhile stepfather-to-be. Laura and Katie's favourite show was *Catfish* and they'd picked up plenty of tips from their time binge-watching it. Yes, Greg may have liked to think we were just nobodies from his past, but my friends and family kept us in the loop enough that he was still very much in our present.

It was a bitter pill to swallow for us as a family, to come to terms with the fact that because of him we were now living very different lives from what we had known. Lives consisting of buy-one-get-one-free, cheap supermarket deals and clothes from charity shops, while he was living it up in the lap of luxury. No 'cheap-arse Fridays' for him, that was for sure. No, he was still enjoying his flash restaurant meals and lavish lifestyle all documented in detail on Instagram. Exotic trips away to St Lucia and Spain to name but a few. It was clear he was very much still living the high life with his ever-loving girlfriend.

He may have been quaffing champagne whilst we drank cheap chardonnay, but we took comfort in knowing he was on borrowed time. He couldn't evade justice forever, and we would often raise a glass of low-cost plonk and toast his inevitable downfall. The drink might have been as rough as hell on the tastebuds, but it tasted sweet in that moment. Yes, his downfall couldn't come soon enough for us all.

And here we were now, sitting in our warm homes, albeit in lockdown, knowing that he was sitting in a cold, uncomfortable cell. That Friday toast with our budget wine so long ago coming to fruition.

14

The Little Boy With No Name

Karen and I continued our trip down memory lane, both scribbling down page after page of notes for the timeline. There was so much to go over. A big part of it was the difficulties I encountered some two years after Greg had run off. At the time, mentally and physically, I was in a much better place. I had a part time job, Charlie was thriving in nursery and I had met Scott. We had a new family – a real family.

I knew that a family holiday would be just what we all needed. Nothing fancy, just a cheap package deal somewhere in the sun. No St Lucia, for us but Lanzarote would be just the thing. No one could deny that we all deserved a break away after the last few years. It was decided that myself, Scott, Charlie, Scott's sons, Karen, Ryan, Mum and Yvonne would all go away together and make some new, happy memories. However, that turned out to be a lot easier said than done.

Initially after Greg first left, I had gone to see a solicitor, desperate to have Charlie's name changed. There was no 'James Scott' , so therefore there could be no 'Charlie Scott'. My little boy's name was fake, his surname from a father who, in reality, never existed.

My solicitor was aghast. He scratched his head, pondering on what to suggest. He had never seen anything like it before in his career and unfortunately was at a complete loss as to what he could do. An official entry on a Birth Register is binding and not something that can just be changed. Therefore, the only thing that he could suggest was a 'Statutory Declaration for change of surname for a child'. This was not ideal by any means, but it would have to do.

It did mean I would be able to change Charlie's surname for nursery, the doctors, dentists etc. So, with my mum kindly offering to pay the solicitor's fees, that was what I decided to do. Charlie became known, from then on, as Charlie Ferguson, mine and Karen's surname at birth, and his grandma's surname. It was a comfort too for Mum, for her name to continue on.

Armed with Charlie's new surname, I excitedly applied for his first passport. I was so happy the surname Scott was a thing of the past for my little boy and felt confident that everything was now sorted. How naïve was I to think that? Greg's parting legacy – the name Scott was going nowhere.

I sighed deeply as Karen and I talked in depth about the pain and difficulties I had to endure just trying to get that passport for Charlie. It was like continually banging my head against a brick wall. Everyone I talked to at the Passport Office was so sympathetic to my situation but at a loss as to what to do to help. They had never encountered this situation before, and time and time again I was told that the only way Charlie's passport could be issued in a name differing from the Birth Certificate was with a letter of authority from the child's biological father, as stated on the birth certificate. The one and only 'James Scott'.

I lost count of the times I pleaded with staff down the phone, explaining repeatedly that this was impossible. How could I get permission from a man who did not exist? Had never existed. They were quite literally asking for the impossible. The passport staff were helpful, but their hands were tied. It was escalated to the higher echelons but still to no avail. My solicitor's declaration, in this instance, was not worth the paper it was written on.

Everyone wanted to help, but there was no way around it. Charlie was 'Charlie Scott', pure and simple, and that was the only passport that could be issued.

"It was utter madness if you think about it, Karen," I stated, shaking my head at her down the computer screen. "I was honest and transparent about everything, but the only way I could take Charlie away on a holiday was to take him under a fake surname, all with the full knowledge of the authorities."

So as there was no other choice, that is what we had to do. Nine of us travelled on that week away to sunny Lanzarote. Little Charlie with his brand-new passport, bearing a name that didn't match mine or Scott's.

"The bloody hassle that caused too," Karen muttered. "The way we got treated, the suspicion – it's no flaming surprise you haven't taken him abroad since."

It had been traumatic. We had been stopped at Border control, questioned with raised eyebrows, regarded with wariness. I totally understand why the authorities can't be too careful, but once again I had to explain my story, why my child's name was different from mine. I had to prove who I was, who Charlie was, recount the whole sorry tale, yet again. I had to see the shocked faces of disbelief, repeatedly. I really should have been used to it by now. I appreciated why this had to happen, but it didn't stop me feeling like some sort of criminal. I was questioned over and over while Greg could happily sun himself on his luxury holidays, without a care in the world. Well at least for the time being.

I wasn't going to put myself through that harrowing experience again, any time soon. I knew that Scott was keen to adopt Charlie in due course, so comforted myself that at some point in the future, Charlie would bear Scott's surname. He would no longer be the little boy who didn't exist.

We did have little family holidays again after the trip to Lanzarote. My photo album bulging with happy shots of us all on the beach, on funfair rides, eating ice cream. Charlie always in the forefront of these pictures, smiling happily, having the time of his life. All these holidays were in the UK. There might have been no suntans and no travels to exotic destinations, but these getaways in Britain were still wonderful. The people who surround you make your holiday truly special. Even a wet weekend in Bognor Regis.

Bognor Regis would not have been the first choice on Greg's list of desired destinations, so there was definitely no chance of bumping into him there. As we knew only too well, he had a taste for the high life, his extravagant lifestyle dating back many years. Long before he met me.

I had discovered that in his late twenties he had been pensioned off from the Army on the grounds of ill health. He received a generous pension but also a tidy settlement sum of £100,000. This money, Iain had informed us, he had burnt through in little over a year. He had spent the money on fancy cars, jewellery, holidays and memberships at swanky Golf Clubs and Spas for himself and Rachel. Cash doesn't last long when you are living like a millionaire.

Iain, his brother-in-law, had laughed as he told us what a 'pillock' Greg had been, always playing the big man. He had tried his best to lord it over his family, make them feel lesser, but it hadn't worked. In fact, Iain had told us he thought they had both behaved like a couple of jumped-up knobs.

Maybe this is where his desire to be back playing the Flash Harry role began. Perhaps he needed to change everything about himself, reinvent a whole new person. Who knows? What I do know is that Bognor Regis was better off without him.

15

Time Is A Great Healer

After days of tears, laughter and aching hands from all the writing, we finally had our timeline completed. I dread to think how many cups of tea and packets of biscuits we had devoured, but I knew the waistband of my jeans was feeling that little bit tighter. Mind you, in lockdown I think everyone was gaining a few unwanted extra pounds.

It had certainly been quite the journey, reliving that time, and nothing had been left out. Everything was included, from Greg's full-on love bombing of me, to all his lies and frauds. Well, at least the ones we knew about. It was despicable that the man had conned my family, friends and acquaintances, but worst of all was the fact he had conned charities. He had made fake promises. In effect he had stolen from the sick and vulnerable. No one was safe from his greed.

Since he had disappeared from our lives, faded into the shadows like a bad memory, his deceptive behaviour had continued. Iain, our now-friend and Greg's brother-in-law, kept in regular contact via phone calls, messages and occasional visits. Iain and his family were always supportive to us, and we appreciated them all. They were eager for us to get our justice and for Greg to face punishment.

One afternoon, many months before Greg would finally face justice, I was busily chopping vegetables for the evening meal. I was keeping an ever-watchful eye over Charlie who was happily playing with his toy cars on the living room rug. A message had pinged through on my mobile phone. I put down my knife and picked up the device, squinting at the screen – I really needed to invest in a pair of reading glasses. I smiled as I realised it was a message from Iain. It was always nice to hear from him. I opened the message and realised he had sent me some screenshots from a Facebook group he was a member of. It was a charity that supported ex-Army veterans and as he was ex-Army, he followed the group. He had been in complete shock when a post had popped up and, lo and behold, there was a face he had instantly recognised. It was Greg, grinning broadly, against the backdrop of a sunny field, his receding sandy hairline glinting in the sun. And once again he was boasting about how benevolent he was. Good old charitable Greg now owned a smart property with a large plot of land surrounding it. He had posted on the group that he was more than happy for the charity to use this land whenever they needed for camping, teambuilding activities or other outdoor pursuits.

The Facebook group had many members, and they came out in force to congratulate Greg for his selfless generosity, telling him what a wonderful gesture it was. There was gushing praise, respect pouring out through the comments section. It proved his behaviour hadn't stopped at all. He was doing this just to feel like the big man again, lying to a charity, making false promises. Maybe life had gone a bit too quiet and uneventful for him. Perhaps there was not much happening while he was waiting for his next court appearance, and he needed to spice things up, to get his fix by feeling like the hero again. Of course, he did not own a large property with impressive grounds, he was just up to his old tricks again. Iain had immediately contacted the charity himself and set them straight. Whether they took any action against Greg, I don't know. And I don't know how many other charities he was making false promises to. I'm sure there were plenty. At least now he was banged up; charities were safe from his lies… for now.

I neatly stacked the sheets of paper bearing my scribbled ramblings into a pile on the coffee table in front of me. The handwritten timeline ready to give to Jon. I looked at the pages taking in the various coffee stains and random smudges that, most probably, had been due to a rogue tear or two.

I could see my twin sister via my computer screen, neatly stacking up her notes too, finally satisfied that we had completed our task.

"We can't give this to Jon in this state Kazza. How about you type it up nice and neat for when we get to meet him?"

Karen sighed and ran her hand through her brown hair, making it stick up in random tufts. "Well, that's my next few nights sorted, I guess." But deep down I knew she didn't mind. If we were doing this, it needed to be done right.

Jon was due to visit us both at my home the following weekend and Karen was going to travel the 50 miles to see us. We would have to meet up in my back garden, socially distanced, but it was important. He really wanted to meet us both, put faces to the details he already had and get a feel for us as sisters – how our personalities gelled, how close we both were.

The weather had been unseasonably sunny and warm for the time of year. I was still conscious, though, that it was April and British weather can be very unpredictable. We might get caught in a down pour. I knew if that happened, we would just sit, talk, and get soggy and rained on. A bit of water wasn't going to stop us. However, thankfully, the following Saturday was a dry day. Jon had arrived about lunchtime. I had heard his car approaching as I had been peering nervously out of my front window, expecting his arrival. When he had jumped out of his car, I signalled for him to walk around the side of the house to gain access to the back garden where I had chairs already waiting.

Jon was in his early fifties. A friendly, pleasantly handsome man. Maybe five-foot-ten with slightly greying hair, he was dressed smart yet casual in dark jeans and a checked shirt. From the conversations I had already had with him over the phone I had formed an impression in my head, the way you do, of what he might look like. Overall, I was pretty spot on.

Karen had already arrived half an hour earlier. She was looking smarter than I had seen her of late. I was used to seeing her in her pyjamas over our daily Zoom call, and to see her dressed smartly in a floral maxi dress and cropped denim jacket was a pleasant change. She had also applied a little makeup for the occasion. Likewise, I had smartened myself up for meeting Jon. It was nice to have any excuse to make a bit of an effort. We both greeted Jon nervously. There were no handshakes of course but plenty of timid smiles. I made mugs of strong tea for everyone and put out my fanciest biscuits.

"Do you mind if I record our conversation?" Jon asked, already busy laying out a recording device on the table in front of us.

I quickly caught Karen's eye and we both nodded our agreement before we started to talk.

Jon had already had the timeline emailed to him by Karen, but as he said, "there is no substitute to having the story relayed to him, via the victims, in their own words." So that is what we did. We talked for many hours, Jon swept up in the journey of 'James', staggered and amazed, often shaking his head in disbelief. At the end of our conversation, he was even more determined this was a story that needed to be shared.

"Leave it with me," he instructed, gathering all his equipment together, "it might take a bit of time to get it all sorted but I'm excited to make a start. I'll keep in touch and please ring me anytime you need to." He furnished us both with a warm smile.

Karen and I returned his smile. He had been so easy to talk to.

"Don't worry Jon, Karen and I are used to everything in this process taking a long time, we know how to be patient."

"I hope Greg is being patient too." Karen had laughed ruefully. "He's going to need to be, stuck in a prison cell for years to come."

Jon nodded. "Hope it gives him time to think and maybe to change his ways."

I caught Karen's eye again. We both doubted this.

With that, Jon made his way out of the garden giving us a wave as he left. We heard his car pull out of the drive as he headed off on the long journey home.

I turned to my sister. "Well, that seemed to go well. He was a really nice chap, but he's certainly had a lot to take in this afternoon."

She smiled back but I noticed she looked a little pale even under her makeup, and didn't seem quite her usual happy, positive self. She was a little more subdued and just seemed a little weary.

She was probably just overly tired after all the talking, I reasoned with myself. It was a stressful topic and we had talked nonstop for hours.

"You ok sis?" I questioned, my voice heavy with concern. "Are you feeling alright?"

She had given a small shrug. "Just a little tired I guess, a bit out of sorts," she replied. "I'm sure it's nothing. It's been a hell of a few days."

I nodded in agreement. "Get yourself off home now and get your feet up," I urged. "We'll talk more tomorrow. I feel we've turned a corner now. Surely things can only get better for us from now on."

16

One Step Forward Two Steps Back

The weeks rolled past, each day sliding seamlessly into the next, with home schooling and Joe Wick's exercise plans creating some structure to our days. We left Jon to get on with working on the podcast, and knew he would be back in contact with us if and when he needed to.

We all tried to get back to some semblance of normality – or at least as normal as possible whilst the country was still in a national lockdown. Fear and heartbreak were all too much a reality for everyone in their day to day lives. Families were cut off from each other, loved ones unable to even hug, family members tragically passing away from the virus. It was a strange and scary world we were all now forced to exist in.

Karen was still not feeling too well. She was a bit run down but didn't want to make too much of a fuss or bother anyone, especially with an already-stretched NHS.

We still had our frequent catchups on the phone, talking most days, and I couldn't help but feel a little concerned about her. My normal bright and bubbly twin just seemed to have lost her spark. It was like her inner light had been switched off.

"At least give your doctors a ring," I urged, concern clear in my voice. "Talk to someone on the phone. Make an appointment to get your bloods checked, you really don't seem yourself at the moment. You're probably just a little deficient in something, maybe you're anaemic," I suggested. "You likely need a course of vitamins or something to give you a little boost."

I heard her sigh deeply over the phone. "I really don't want to bother them. It's probably nothing, could just be my age. We are now in our 40s Col, and the joys of the dreaded menopause can't be too far away. I'm sure that's the issue. And I've got a bit of a water infection too, which is making me feel really icky and I know they become more frequent at this time in our lives."

I had heard that as well, but still nagged her to make an appointment. She argued that it was impossible to even get through to her GP surgery, they were that overwhelmed, but I was adamant she had to keep trying.

"OK, OK," she eventually promised, although more just to shut me up. "I'll make an appointment but I'm sure I'll be as right as rain in a few days' time."

But she wasn't any better the following day when I called, or on the days that followed. The water infection she hoped was clearing up took hold with a vengeance, and when she then started to pass blood and was in quite a lot of pain, Karen relented and made an appointment with her doctor.

She later told me that as she sat in the nearly-deserted waiting room wearing her requisite facemask, she had felt a little guilty. Worried that she might be wasting the precious time of the nurses and doctors who were already stretched to breaking point. She had been called into a small examination room and after providing a urine sample it was confirmed the next day that she was indeed suffering from a bladder infection and the appropriate course of antibiotics was prescribed.

The Nurse that treated Karen had been extremely thorough. She had told her in a reassuring voice she was sure that once the infection had been dealt with the bleeding would stop. It was probably just caused by irritation to the bladder lining, but to be safe it would be prudent for her to have a cystoscopy, a procedure where a camera is placed into the bladder, and a CT scan. Just to be on the safe side as there had been a fair amount of blood and pain.

"Is that absolutely necessary?" Karen asked, nodding towards the sample bottle still sitting on the cluttered desk in front of her. "I'm sure after a couple of days I'll be fighting fit again. I've had these infections before and I'm sure there's someone more needy that needs those scans more than I do."

The nurse had been adamant that she should have the scans 'just in case'. At the time she hadn't been sure what 'just in case' meant, but in time that would become all too clear.

"You will receive your appointment within the next two weeks," the nurse explained. The poor woman had looked frazzled, her shoulder length blonde hair had springing curls escaping from out of her tight bun and my sister wondered to herself when she had last had a break.

Karen headed out of the surgery clutching her prescription for a short course of broad-spectrum antibiotics to take until the urine sample was analysed and the actual infection confirmed. She had slowly walked into the deserted street beyond. Barely anyone was around these days, it felt eerie and odd. Almost like being in some grim post-apocalyptic horror film, the usual hustle and bustle of humanity now reduced to bleak silence and occasional pieces of litter being tossed around the street by a sudden gust of wind. Most people would already be in their houses, patiently waiting for Boris's evening broadcast and what his new instructions would be. This routine had become second nature to everyone in the country.

The course of antibiotics thankfully did their job and within a couple of days she was starting to feel so much better. She nearly phoned to cancel the scans, but the kindly nurse's words had echoed in her mind, and she decided to err on the side of caution and attend the appointment. After all it would only be an hour or so out of her day.

Thank God she did go for those scans. And if any of our family ever met that wise nurse again, we would hug her and thank her, because her zealousness in insisting that Karen should have scans – "to dot the i-s and cross the t-s" as she had said – could very well have saved my sister's life.

A tumour had been detected in her right kidney measuring almost 10 centimetres. Meaning the whole kidney and adrenal gland needed to be removed as soon as possible. This was essential surgery and time was of the essence. Our whole family was devastated and desperate to be with Karen. To look after and support her. But COVID would, of course, not allow that.

The medics had informed her that although they couldn't confirm that the tumour was cancerous without pathology, they were convinced it was, so the kidney needed to be removed as a matter of priority.

After the past few years we had lived through as a family, how was this fair? Greg often used cancer in his deceptions, to gain sympathy, to allow his frauds to flourish. He said he had cancer himself and he also lied about his mother having breast cancer and having a mastectomy. Neither of them had had cancer, but

Karen did. It was yet another fight for us to face.

She had her surgery alone. Scared and unable to have visits from anyone, desperate to be at home with Ryan, her daughter Emily and her little grandson.

The surgery had gone well. Within a couple of weeks she had been told that the cancer was stage 3 and had been contained within the kidney. If it had been left any longer though, it could have been a very different story. The Doctor stated that she had been very unlucky because kidney cancer was exceedingly rare in non-smoking women, especially at her age with no family history. But as we are more than aware, cancer is cruel and very inclusive. She had just been the unlucky one.

Ryan took time off work to help Karen with her recuperation. Which was not easy as, to top it off, Ryan's mum had passed away just days before Karen received her diagnosis. To add to all the misery, a few weeks later and they both contracted COVID, making Karen's recovery just a little bit more difficult. But little by little Karen got stronger, more positive and her glow was returning.

But nothing could have prepared her, or any of us, for the next cruel blow. A blood test had indicated elevated calcium and PT (parathyroid hormone) levels in Karen's blood and a whole new raft of tests and scans had to be undertaken. Endocrinologists were confident it was a benign tumour on one of her parathyroid glands. These four glands are situated just below the thyroid and regulate calcium levels within the blood.

Karen had surgery to remove two of the glands. No one, least of all her, expected to discover that she had cancer again. But she did. Parathyroid cancer is unbelievably rare. She had joked that it was about as likely as winning the lottery and she knew which one she would have preferred. My poor sister had been through so much – her neck cut open only a few months after her renal surgery to remove her kidney and adrenal gland. Life really did deliver some cruel blows.

17

Glimmer Of Hope

Despite this terrible news, life went on its usual way, as it invariably does. The months rolled by slowly, the whole country, indeed the entire world, still in lockdown. Summer heat made way for crisp autumn days and then into the sharp chill of winter. Before we knew it, Christmas was upon us once again.

The 'powers that be' in Downing Street thankfully relented and announced that families could meet again, if they must, but only for Christmas Day and whilst taking as many precautions as humanly possible. Facemasks were to be worn where possible, windows kept open to ventilate rooms, a decent space maintained between relatives. We didn't need telling twice. Nothing was going to stop our family from coming together after the last year, celebrating the fact that we were all still here and stronger, despite everything we had all been through.

I was hosting Christmas dinner at our house. I had, of course, ordered way too much food and drink, but I didn't care. So what if I had bought three different types of chutney for the cheeseboard? I wanted everything to be perfect, to be a day everyone would remember. It was going to be quite a squeeze however, my kitchen not particularly big and my smart round table now had the addition of a pasting table jutting out from the end. There was a mix of chairs, including some garden furniture that Scott had given a good clean. But I knew no one would care about where they sat.

I smiled to myself proudly as I put the finishing touches to the kitchen table. The glasses were sparkling, and the festive tablecloth looked so jolly with its holly and mistletoe design. It was Christmas Eve evening. Charlie was jumping up and down, barely able to contain his excitement. He was desperate to get himself involved with the preparations. He had made little place cards for all the guests. They had his scribbly writing on them and were cutely adorned with sequins, glitter and lopsided Christmas trees. He followed me around like my little shadow, thoughtfully deciding where everyone should sit and putting the appropriate card down at each place. I, of course, would rearrange them all later once he had gone to bed. I would then have to also get out my old trusty vacuum cleaner and attempt to remove all the evidence of glitter from my carpets. It had spread everywhere in the house, even in the fur of our two pussy cats. They were very festive felines this year.

I sighed inwardly. No doubt I would still be clearing the glitter come February. Charlie's excited little voice snapped me out of my thoughts. He was clearly bubbling over with glee, and I couldn't help but smile at my son. His excitement really was infectious.

"Do you think Santa is going to be here soon Mum?" His little cheeks were slightly flushed, and he had dried smears of chocolate around his mouth from the chocolate snowman I had allowed him to have earlier. "I hope he doesn't get too tired, he has so far to travel. Do you think he stops for a little nap at all?"

His face had taken on a worried look. He was clearly concerned about old Saint Nick's responsibilities. "He doesn't want to be late and have Mrs Claus up waiting for him, worrying."

I laughed and scooped my little boy up into my arms for a cuddle. Only he was not so little anymore. In fact, in just a couple of months my Charlie Bear would be turning five years old. Now in Reception class at school, he was really flourishing and making me so proud every day. A "kind and conscientious little boy" his teachers announced, and they were absolutely spot on. He really had come so far from the dark days after his father's disappearance.

"Don't you be fretting," I reassured him gently, as I gave him another cuddle. "Santa knows exactly what he's doing, and he really doesn't need to stop for a nap. He's got so much energy from all the lovely treats left in all of the houses." I ruffled my son's blonde hair so it was sticking up in cute random tufts. "And that's exactly what we need to sort out now, what treats we leave for Santa. Once that's done we need to get you tucked up into bed young man, and get some sleep. Santa doesn't want sleepy boys and girls opening their presents tomorrow morning." I took this opportunity to plant a little kiss on the top of my son's head.

"Mince pies and a small glass of sherry for Santa and carrots for his reindeers," I told Charlie with a decisive nod of my head. "That's what Santa likes, so that is what we're going to leave for him."

Charlie jumped out of my embrace with a whoop of glee and dashed off to find the special Christmas treat plastic plate we had bought the previous week for the Big Man's arrival. It most certainly is true what people say, Christmas is magical when you have little ones around.

The following morning Scott and I were dragged out of bed at 6am by Charlie, whether we wanted to be or not. My son steadfastly refused to stay in his bed a single second longer. We followed him down the stairs sleepily, rubbing the sleep from our eyes and yawning as we went. But truthfully, we were nearly as excited about the day ahead as little Charlie was.

In previous years Karen had always been the one to host on Christmas Day. Loving to open her home up to everyone, enjoying the fuss and making wonderful memories. But it was not to be this year. Karen was doing really well, in no small part due to her positive mindset and cheerful disposition, and of course her ongoing care and support from Ryan, the rest of the family and the wonderful NHS.

My sister was still recuperating and was very tired and rather run down most of the time. She was not only struggling with her health, but with their finances too. She was unable to work now, due to her health. Since she had been forced into bankruptcy by Greg's actions, times were really tough. They had been living through hard times before her diagnosis, but were now literally living from one day to the next.

The Christmas dinner had been a huge success, even if the jars of chutney remained unopened. Buckles and waistbands had been undone and there were groans of "I couldn't eat another bite" and "I'm fit to burst" ringing out from around the table. As I cleared away the Christmas pudding dishes Ryan pulled his chair out from the table, its wooden legs scraping along the tiled floor. Once he was on his feet, he refilled his wine glass and raised it high in the air.

"Great meal that Coleen, you certainly give old Gordon Ramsay a run for his money." He gave me a good-natured wink.

"Now that we are all together though, I just want to make a little toast. It's been quite the struggle for us all," he paused for a second to compose himself, clear he was near to tears. "But we're all still here, and together, and that is to be celebrated. Family is all that really matters." And with a "cheers" he lifted his glass aloft.

The accompanying "cheers" from everyone resonated around the table, everyone happy and smiling. All of us together, strong and supportive.

"And here's to good old 'James' or 'Greg' or maybe it's 'Walter Mitty' now." Ryan laughed. "I hope he is enjoying his Christmas lunch at Her Majesty's Pleasure, and I hope his turkey is dry and his sprouts are burnt."

"To Walter Mitty," we all sang out, "may his sprouts be burnt." We all turned to each other clinking our glasses together.

Laughter and happiness filled my house that day. Not even Greg could spoil that.

Lockdown continued on. The weeks merging into months, every day like the one before. It really was like Groundhog Day. It was Thursday, 8th April 2021. Exactly a year to the very day from Greg's sentencing. Although I was aware of the date, it was just another day for me. I was sitting on the sofa staring at the news on the widescreen TV in the corner of the room, slowly chewing on my boring cheese sandwich, wishing I had added a bit of pickle to it, when between bites I opened the Facebook app on my phone to have a little bit of a nosy.

"Lee Walker has tagged you and others into a post," it had announced to me in the notifications section. With a smile I clicked on the link, eager to see what it was. I liked Lee. We may have met through Greg's lies and cons, but he had always

supported us, been a really good supportive friend.

This time, however, it wasn't a joke or funny meme. It was a news article from that day's Newcastle Chronicle. Greg Wilson had, unbeknown to us, been back in Court. Because of his crimes he had been ordered, under the Proceeds of Crime Bill, to pay £36,000 in compensation. He had so many victims, but it was deemed that I was the principal one, so from his Army pension he would have to pay me £1000 a month for the next 36 months.

I stared, dumbfounded, at my phone screen, having to reread the article over and over again just for it to finally sink it. I had no idea that this was even happening. That he was even due to attend Court again. No one had contacted me. I only knew now as it had appeared on Facebook and thankfully Lee had tagged me into the article. But I didn't care. This was amazing, really amazing. Of course, I knew this was none of Greg's doing. It must have really hurt him to realise he was going to have to pay further for his crimes. I didn't care. In truth, the fact he was being forced into it made it even sweeter. I trotted into the kitchen to get some chutney for my sandwich. To hell with it, I was going to have a big slice of cake too, to celebrate.

18

Still Pulling The Strings

I felt like such a weight had been lifted from my shoulders. This money would make all the difference to Karen and Ryan, as I planned on giving half to them. It would give them one less thing to worry about, a little less stress, and I couldn't wait to tell them. The only concerning element was the comments aimed at Greg that I was reading at the foot of the article. Quite a few messages had been left from people who had obviously encountered Greg Wilson before. I felt prickles of anxiety as I read them.

PastaPasta

I had the unfortunate experience of playing a round of golf with this shady character, not only was I gobsmacked at the tales this thing told, he also tried to get me involved with one of his many business ventures – his charms did not work on this old horse, a dangerous piece of work he is.

Phahahahahaha

Yes, I've seen this cretin at friends' family parties but sure he went by the name of Ian, always was a dirty sleaze.

RichardTricky

Oh no, Durham Police, his lies did not start in 2017 they started long, long ago...I am so glad to see this man brought to book!

ChrisDonnelly

I met up with him, was an old army mate. Told me he was a teacher in Stockton driving around in a brand-new Porsche. Shocked and disappointed to see that someone can actually do this to someone.

BarbaraLawrence

He used to date my friend, met her off POF a few years back, he seemed strange then.

Chris652

Trust me, you know when Greg Wilson is lying - his mouth is moving.

How long had Greg been using dating sites whilst married, or trying to manipulate people into his cons? These were just a few comments I had stumbled on, as I now avoided the internet as much as possible. I had been burnt before, felt the sting of harsh words from anonymous strangers, so I tried not to open myself up to that pain again. But how many more people were out there that Greg Wilson had hurt? I dreaded to think.

I closed the article down and pushed my phone away from me so I wouldn't be tempted to have another look. It was pointless torturing myself. I would never know how many victims there actually were. I needed to concentrate on the bit of good news I had heard today. I plodded into the kitchen to make myself a cup of tea because I knew my next conversation may be a long one. Returning to the sofa a few minutes later, steaming mug in hand, I reached again for my mobile phone and dialled Karen's number. After a few rings, the call connected. Karen was as lovely as ever, but lately her voice always just seemed that little bit flatter. Her humour and often sarcastic wit were not so forthcoming anymore. Her sparkle had dimmed, and it was sorely missed by everyone, especially me. I really hoped my news would put a much-needed smile back onto her face.

"You'll never guess what has just happened?" I gushed, eager to get my words out and not even giving her a chance to reply. "Greg's been back in Court today. The little git is being forced to pay his Army pension to me each month to the tune of..." I paused for a few seconds to build a little tension and drama before announcing, "£36,000!"

I heard the sharp intake of breath on the other end of the line. "W... what... really?" Karen sounded as stunned as I had expected her to be. "I can't believe it, is it really true?"

"It certainly is," I confirmed, the delight in my voice evident. "He's had his bed and board paid for the last year, and for the next two coming, so it's not like he needs the money. And let's face it, how would that be fair if he left prison with the best part of £40,000 burning a hole in his back pocket from his Army pension? Out and about with all that cash to go along his merry way." I paused for a few seconds before continuing more seriously. "In my eyes he's still getting away lightly, only serving half a sentence. For what he did he should serve the full six years."

I continued to tell my sister that although the compensation was to be awarded to me, I didn't want a penny of it. Yes, I had lost my job because of Greg, but in my eyes, I had a much better one now – being Charlie's mum – and I was happy. Money was never what Greg had stolen from me and I certainly didn't want any of his money now. I wanted nothing from that man, absolutely nothing. I decided that anything I received would be split 50/50 – half of it would be put aside for Charlie and his future, he was the most innocent victim of all, and half would be given to Karen. It would not even make a dent in the amount that Greg had taken from her, but at this moment in time it would be a much-needed lifeline. I think that afternoon on that call was the first time I could hear a bit of the old Karen coming back to us. I shouldn't have been naïve though. I should have realised that anything connected to Greg would never be straightforward.

Nothing to do with him was ever without a fight. The following four months passed without a single penny dropping into my bank account from the Criminal Fines Collection Agency. I checked daily, hating the neediness in my actions. I hated the fact that Karen was relying on this money, but that once again Greg was toying with us all. I made so many calls to the Collection Agency, even contacting my MP in desperation to see if they could help at all. I despised the way victims could still be treated in such a way. His case was recalled to Court and thankfully payments then did start. Whilst he was in prison, he really couldn't wriggle out of making payments and honouring the Court order. The £36,000 was to cover the 36 months he was locked up. He didn't need this money so it was felt appropriate that he should compensate his victims. However, he was already 16 months into his sentence, this debt would spill well over after his release date – many, many thousands of pounds still owing. We were all well aware that Greg was not known for honouring his debts, so he had no doubt played the system again. He was always the one pulling the strings. Despite all this there was still good news. Some money was better than none. And seeing this money help Karen over the months to come, witness her getting stronger and Greg being hit where it hurt him the most

– in his pocket – was reason enough to celebrate.

19

Come Back Fighting

We were now in late Summer 2021. We had thankfully just emerged from the country's second national lockdown. Scott and I had made the decision that the time was right to forge ahead with the adoption process. It was so important to us both for Charlie to have a true sense of belonging, not to mention a real, forever name with his real, forever dad. Scott had already tried previously to get the ball rolling, filling forms in online to start the adoption of a stepchild. He had also been in contact with our local Council. Unfortunately, the process had been halted, completely stopped in its tracks. Home visits were imperative in compiling the report and because of lockdown these could not take place. Understandably we had been disappointed, but we were determined to keep trying. Now the second lockdown had been lifted, Scott wasted no time in applying again.

This time a case file was opened and excitedly we started the long journey to Charlie's existence being acknowledged by society. No longer with a fake name but instead with our family name.

We had several home visits with our lovely case appointed Social Worker, Dawn. A smiley young woman with a shock of wavy auburn hair. Charlie had taken a shine to her instantly and loved when she would tell him all about her two dogs, who sounded exceedingly mischievous. Dawn also went to visit my sister-in-law, Mel, and Yvonne who we had appointed as our referees. So many questions were asked and so many forms had to be completed, but we didn't mind a jot. We were just so happy things were finally moving head. And they were, until it all sadly ground to a halt yet again.

Dawn had sat on the edge of her chair, concern etched across her face as she spoke. "I'm so very sorry to have to tell you this." She sighed deeply before continuing, her voice heavy with emotion. "I know it's really unfair, but my hands are tied."

Scott and I turned to face her, worried what we could be about to hear.

Social Workers need to be impartial in all cases, but I was well aware of the fact that Dawn had been rooting for our family one hundred percent. She knew how much Charlie loved Scott and how happy we were as a family. It was clear that the news she had to impart to us was genuinely upsetting for her too.

"Your case has been escalated because of the issues with the biological father's name." She sighed as she continued. "You know we've never dealt with this type of situation before."

Memories of my many conversations with the Passport Office came flooding back to me. I felt my breath catch in my throat. I couldn't believe we were going to have to go through all this again.

It had been decided that, even though Scott was clearly now Charlie's dad, and they were devoted to each other, that continuing with this application would prove a costly and futile exercise. Once it was placed in front of the Judge in Family Court for the Adoption Order, the Judge would disregard it and throw the whole case out. The biological father's name was Greg Wilson but that did not match the 'James Scott' named on Charlie's birth certificate. And for that very reason the Judge would not take things any further.

I cried buckets that afternoon, until my face was red and bloated. I couldn't believe the sheer injustice of it all. Charlie, a true innocent, but once again suffering because of the cruel actions of Greg.

"Well, that's it. We're beaten," I ranted at Scott once my tears had finally abated and the inevitable anger had taken hold. I threw my hands up in the air. "That cowardly piece of shit has won again. He's still the one in control. What's the bloody point of even trying? It always feels like the deck is stacked in his favour." I sighed defeatedly and sunk down further into my seat. "It's just one battle after a bloody 'nother."

I felt totally exhausted. I wasn't even angry anymore. What was the point? The only person I really wanted to vent my anger at was Greg and I hadn't clapped eyes on him in over five years. Scott tentatively sat down on the sofa next to me and gently took my hand in his.

"Look at me Col," he urged, softly. I turned and looked into his kind, brown eyes. The eyes of the man I loved. "Be honest, if there is one thing you're used to through all of this, it is having to fight. You've not shied away from it before and this time it's for Charlie. Plus, I've got your back now and I'm going nowhere. I promise we'll get this sorted."

He squeezed my hand tightly and I gave him a big hug, holding on for a long time. He really was my rock. He was right of course; it was just another fight I needed to have. So fight I did.

Firstly, I contacted the Registry Office and, as expected, faced the same barriers I had encountered previously at the Passport Office. There was nothing they could do, I was once again told. They really sympathised, wished they could help, but they just couldn't. I refused to be beaten. I contacted my MP, the Courts and, in desperation, DC Chris Bentham. If anyone knew just how much Greg had made my family suffer it was Chris, and he was ready to step in and fight with me.

He had argued back and forth with the Registry Office. He produced facts from the case – anything and everything that could sway their decision in his quest to help us.

When I read one of the emails I was copied into, I couldn't help but smile. Chris was obviously getting as frustrated as I was.

"For God's sake do you not think she's suffered enough? Give the poor girl a break," he had fired off. I couldn't have put it better myself.

Somehow it worked! No, the Birth Certificate could not be altered – that wasn't up for discussion – but the Powers that Be decided a footnote could be added to the certificate recognising that 'James Scott' was the name also used by Greg Wilson. Not ideal but I prayed that it would be enough to help. When I informed Dawn, she had agreed that it was enough. The case file stated that Greg Wilson was Charlie's biological father, and if that name appeared on the Birth Certificate in some format too, it would be enough to go before the Judge. So, for the third time, we started the adoption process. And thankfully, the third time really was the charm.

We still experienced many more hurdles along the way, caused by none other than Mr Greg Wilson. He legally needed to be informed of the adoption and given his right to respond to it, whether he would agree or if his intention was to fight it.

A notification was sent to the Prison that Greg was now languishing in – Kirk Levington Grange, a category D open prison near Yarm in North Yorkshire. He didn't respond. We hadn't expected him to. It was Greg, after all. We left it for many weeks but heard nothing. We didn't want to leave anything to chance so we had the letter sent once again, but this time by solicitor. That meant that it needed a signature as confirmation of receipt. We needed proof that Greg had actually received the letter because we didn't trust him not to lie and say that he had never got it. Again, weeks passed with still no response. It didn't surprise me. Of course Charlie was of no importance or interest to the man whatsoever, and that suited me down to the ground. Without a response from him within a certain time the adoption application could be submitted, and a hearing date scheduled. I couldn't stop smiling. I could finally see the end in sight. Charlie would no longer be the little boy with no name.

As is normal, the Court appointed their own CAFCAS Social Worker to do their own independent review, and she too came to do a home visit on the run up to the hearing.

The rainy Friday morning she arrived I opened my front door eagerly, warmly inviting her into our home.

"Hi, I'm June," she announced, shaking my hand and returning my welcoming smile. She briskly removed her soaking raincoat as I took her umbrella from her to dry in the kitchen. She followed closely behind me and once we were in the living room, I gestured for her to sit down. Scott busied himself in the kitchen making tea and plating up biscuits. Scott always believed in the merits of a good cup of tea when important matters needed to be discussed.

June was a neatly dressed woman in her mid-fifties. She was

pleasant and chatty and we engaged in a little small talk to start with. She thanked Scott as she accepted her mug of tea and smiled, eager to start the conversation proper. "I come bearing good news," she announced, helping herself to a chocolate biscuit from the plate Scott was holding. "I've just spoken to Greg on the phone. What a lovely man he is, the poor thing. This adoption is really breaking his heart. It hurts him so much to lose Charlie, but he fully consents to it. He knows it's the right thing to do for his son and he believes that Charlie is the only one that really matters in all of this."

20

Good Old Greg

I couldn't help but gawp at June's happy smiling face. I was totally lost for words. Surely this couldn't be true? Twice Scott and I had tried to get any kind of response from Greg, paid hundreds of pounds to a solicitor in the process, and twice we had failed. One call from June though, and apparently he was once again playing 'Mr Nice Guy', putting Charlie first no matter what pain it was causing him. Selflessly doing the right thing. I couldn't believe my ears and couldn't believe that anyone could still fall for this act. But I did know better than anyone, how convincing and sincere he could appear. He could turn on the charm like he was turning on a light switch.

"He must still think about his son, clearly just wanting what's best for little Charlie," June added. It could have been my imagination, but I thought I saw a tear well up in her eye.

When she said this, my anger bubbled up inside me and I rolled my eyes at the woman. I could keep my exasperation in check no longer.

"Cares for Charlie?" I laughed, bitterly, my voice hard and not at all like me. "He hasn't contacted him in years, hasn't shown a single second's interest in him, never sent even one birthday card. The man is an out-and-out liar and completely full of shit." I was now out of my seat; I could sit still no longer, blood pounding in my ears. "I can't believe you've fallen for his lies. He doesn't care one hoot for Charlie, never has."

I knew I wasn't being fair. Looking at June's face and the shock plastered across it, I suddenly felt sympathy for the woman and angry I had let myself get so riled up. Of course she had been sucked in, we all had been in the past. I just felt sick to my stomach that even after all this time, even from his prison cell, he was still just so believable in his lies.

I apologised to June, of course. I hadn't been fair to the woman. Now much calmer I actually realised that the fact Greg had acquiesced to the adoption was fabulous news. This would make everything run so much more smoothly. But it still troubled me that suddenly he was being so agreeable, giving us exactly what we wanted. Why? What was he up to? Did he have an agenda? I just couldn't believe he was agreeing to the adoption out of the goodness of his heart. To believe he was, for once, putting his son first was a stretch for me. I knew the man too well. But maybe June was right, and he was doing the right thing for once. Perhaps there was a spark of decency somewhere in him.

As we waved June goodbye, and she opened her umbrella once again to make the short, rainy walk to her car, I felt my spirits lifting. Scott shut the front door firmly and locked it. It was just the family again, and that suited me fine. I turned to face my husband, noting that he looked a little pale and tired. I knew the last few months had been taking a toll on him too.

"Do you think on some level Greg is finally trying to make amends? Do the right thing by us?"

Scott rubbed my arm and gave a long, weary sigh. "Not a chance." His voice was flat and defeated. "From what I've heard about that man he does nothing out of the goodness of his heart. There's got to be something in it for him."

Two days later we had our answer, and of course Scott had been absolutely right.

Greg was agreeing to the adoption for a valid reason but unfortunately that reason was neither Charlie's wellbeing, nor my happiness. It was, however, a reason that made perfect sense to him. He would agree to the adoption so he could play the good guy again, show he was actually a caring father , or at least give the illusion he was to the general public.

I received a phone call from Jon Douglas. He was in high spirits. He had received good news. The BBC had loved his idea and were keen to commission a podcast about our story. They thought it would be fascinating to delve into the mindset of Greg, his backstory, paint the whole intricate picture and raise awareness to help other victims. The BBC had concurred with Jon in agreeing that it truly was a fascinating story, and they were convinced listeners would think so too.

Of course, Greg had a 'right to reply'. To tell his side of the story in his own words. So, with that in mind, Jon had contacted him in prison via letter but never had a response. He had also phoned Greg's girlfriend giving her an opportunity to speak too. She had given Jon short shrift. She told him angrily that she had no intention whatsoever of being on the podcast and he was never to contact her again. With that she had abruptly terminated the call, well and truly hammering the point home.

It was disappointing that she wasn't going to be involved, but I couldn't say that I was surprised. As his victim I knew only too well how much courage it took to stand tall and speak the truth. However, that wasn't true of her. She still believed his lies, lapped up all his wild stories even though we and the Police had told her the truth. But then again, I had to cut her a little slack; Greg was a master manipulator. Hadn't June the social worker just been sucked in completely by him and his fake charm? He could make you feel like you were the most important person in the world, like a spotlight shone only on you, and only he could realise your true worth. I now knew he had spent his life doing this to women. He would say to me that I was the only person alive that could ever truly hurt him. He would wake suddenly from nightmares, crying out in the dark, dreaming that I had left him or fallen out of love with him. I had needed to comfort him, tell him that he was the only man for me and that we would always be together. I really did feel like I was the centre of his universe.

Greg liked to grab my hand and squeeze it when we were out and about together, and if I didn't squeeze his hand in return immediately, his face would crumple and he would demand to know why I hadn't reciprocated. What was wrong with me? And again, I would have to reassure him and calm his fears. Now I see this for what it really is – control. But I believed every word he said. I believed that Charlie and I were his everything and no doubt he had convinced his girlfriend now that she was too.

Unsurprisingly, over the coming months, Jon never received any response from Greg about appearing on the podcast. But we were in no doubt that he knew that his crimes and lies were soon going to be broadcast to the public, unfolding in compulsive snappy episodes. His girlfriend had surely spoken to him about it too, and we knew he would not have been happy. The only bargaining chip he no doubt felt that he still had was to give the illusion of being a good guy and caring father. That's when he finally agreed to the adoption, claiming to the social worker that it was breaking his heart, but he was putting Charlie first as that was the right thing to do. No matter how much it was hurting him. He was trying once again to play the hero, tip the scales in his favour with public opinion.

I, for one, was not falling for any of it. I was angry at myself for having given him the benefit of the doubt, believing he might actually be doing the right thing by Charlie. And angry that he was using the child he had no interest in as a pawn to try and make himself appear noble. But of course, it was only ever Greg that mattered to Greg. Everyone else was simply collateral damage.

So, a ten-part podcast series had been commissioned with me, Karen, Ryan, Greg's wife Rachel, and Chris Bentham being actively involved. There were other victims and charities that would also have an opportunity to tell their side of the story. Tell how they had been charmed, manipulated and defrauded.

The life and times of 'James Scott', AKA Greg Wilson, would now be laid bare for the entire world to digest. Not only would his actions be questioned, but more importantly, a question would be asked. Why? Why had he done it? What made him tick? Was there anyone who could give any sort of explanation of his bizarre behaviour? The court had been unable to shed any light on his motivation. It really would make one fascinating podcast series, of that there was no doubt.

Jon had a few ideas of who he would like to narrate the story and interview the victims, feeling it needed to be a female voice and ideally someone from the North East of England, as that is where the crimes were committed and where I had lived. Someone who would come across as warm and relatable. The front runner was Vicky Pattison, herself no stranger to failed romances and heartbreak, although nothing on this scale. Vicky was an advocate for women's rights and their empowerment, and it was felt she would be a perfect fit for the message we wanted to put across – that despite being victims we were not going to hide away. We were going to tell our story and hopefully help others.

There was, however, a lot involved in producing the series. Everyone involved was conscious that, although Greg had been given a six year prison sentence, he would only be required to serve three in prison and would be out on licence for the remaining three. Come January 2023 he would be at large again in the world. It was a scary thought. Maybe he would put his crimes behind him having found redemption behind bars, become a model citizen? But I highly doubted it. One thing was for sure though, this podcast needed to be out in time for his release. A warning to other potential victims and a 'welcome on your release from prison' gift to dear old Greg. That thought really did make me smile. It was nice to finally be smiling again.

21

A Voice To Help

Despite everything that had happened in our lives there was one truth that always remained – how strong we were as a family. We were an unbreakable unit. We had certainly been tested, but it would take more than a grubby, lying thief to divide us and tear us apart. I know that Greg had seriously underestimated our strength, our tenacity in bringing him to justice. He had always believed we would crumble under the embarrassment and humiliation, hide away and lick our wounds, lose our faith in humanity. He couldn't have been more wrong. He really had meddled with the wrong family this time.

"You know what you need to do? Write a book, you and Karen together," Ryan had insisted one evening when he and Karen had visited us in Yorkshire to enjoy our wonderful company and an even better local Chinese takeaway. Ryan helped himself to a huge portion of chicken Chow Mein as he continued speaking. "Look at the success of the timeline you wrote for Jon. It really helped you both getting it all out. Seriously there was no stopping the two of you once you got started."

He wasn't wrong. It had really helped focus my mind after the many hateful comments I had received online. I knew Karen had felt it a release too, talking about everything in such depth. But write a book? Neither Karen nor I were authors. Karen had always loved to write as a child and often said, in another lifetime, she would have loved to be an author but she had never gone down that path and that was not the life she was now living. Could we actually write a book? Something that people would want to read? Or would it be a complete disaster? Yes, it was the family's in-joke that we could write a book about what happened to us or make a Hollywood movie. The plot was so farfetched it would seriously give *The Tinder Swindler* a run for its money. But that had all been talk, wishful thinking. We had never, for a second, been serious.

"As if anyone would actually buy it." I rolled my eyes at him as I settled down at the kitchen table to tuck into my char siu curry. I was touched by Ryan's faith in us. He was always championing us. But realistically I felt convinced that if we wrote our story, we would only sell a handful of copies to friends and family and that would be that. We would write a book that would soon fade into obscurity. But maybe we still should? It would be a good way to document everything that we had been through.

"Of course people would buy it," Ryan insisted, his kind face determined. "And you'll have written a book, and how many people can say that? Plus, it will do you good, be cathartic." He paused at this point and his face broke into a wide grin, little pieces of prawn cracker stuck in his beard. "Just imagine if you got it completed for Greg's release from prison next January. What a late Christmas pressie what would be for him."

Karen reached over and brushed the pieces of cracker from her husband's beard. "Not sure if that would be a Chrimbo pressie he would really want. Greggie boy would be happier with a Terry's chocolate orange and a nice pair of socks."

I couldn't help but laugh out loud at this. But the truth was, I would love to see Greg's face if we did write a book. But then again there was a lifetime injunction, and hopefully that would keep him away, so I would just have to imagine his expression. But a book about what he was and what he did to us would be a way for us to take some control. And Greg always loved to be the main man, the centre of attention. I really doubted, though, that this was what he had in mind. That just made the proposition of our story even sweeter.

Karen was very much of the same opinion as me. She had doubts whether anyone would be interested in reading any book we would write. We weren't celebrities, after all. Just two run-of-the-mill, middle aged mums. Yes, we had been through the wringer and then some, been really battered down, that couldn't be denied. But many people had lived through a lot worse and survived to tell their tale. We were lucky, grateful for what we still had – our family's love, our friends and a lot of laughs chucked in for good measure. Material possessions were neither here nor there. We knew what really mattered in life. Money could be made or lost and as long as you had food in your belly and a roof over your head, everything else was just gravy.

As we sat around my kitchen table, plates of half-eaten food congealing by the minute, we discussed the pros and cons of writing the book. Would it be too triggering and emotional for us to live it all again? Karen and I were confident it would not. There was also the cost implication. We would self-publish but there would still be costs involved and none of us had much money. But Ryan was adamant and wouldn't let the subject drop. He talked and talked about the merits of us writing our story in our own words.

"It is so important for people to know your truth," he insisted. "You two have been through so much but you're still a pair of awesome, if not annoying, women. Your positivity is an inspiration, even if you can't see it yourselves."

Karen playfully punched her husband in the arm, and we all laughed.

"Oi you, I'm always awesome and never ever annoying," she quipped, giving him an affectionate smile and cracking open her fortune cookie. "But I don't know Ryan. You are biased because you love us, I don't want to set me and Col up for an almighty fall."

He was having none of this, dispelling all our fears as if they were nothing. He really had great faith in us. He reached over and took Karen's hand. "Are you ok my love?" He had spotted that his wife had unshed tears collecting in her eyes, ready to tumble down her cheeks.

She gestured towards the broken cookie in her hand, the little bit of paper clearly visible amongst the fragments of biscuit. Ryan took it from her gently and read it aloud. "Happier days are definitely ahead for you. The struggle has ended."

Ryan turned her hand over and planted a kiss on it. "Well, that's the wisdom of the fortune cookie and no one can argue with that. You're going to write this book and whether you sell ten copies or ten thousand, it's going to be a great achievement for you."

He was not alone. My daughters, Scott and the rest of the family, Mum included, agreed with him, encouraging us just to go for it.

"What have you got to lose?" That was the question we heard

time and time again from everyone. They were all right. We had already lost so much and this wouldn't be losing, This would be taking back.

And so it was decided, that night at my house, that my sister and I would write our book. There was only so many enthusiastic nudges and so much encouragement and downright nagging we could put up with before we threw in the towel and relented.

And , maybe they were right? This would be a good thing to do. I was worried that when Greg was released his criminal behaviour would just carry on. More misery awaiting many more families. It would be good to leave a legacy, a warning to others. To stop him in his tracks or, at the very least, make his deceptions as difficult for him as we could.

Also, I had an important message for others. After what had happened to me it would have been so easy to call time on all future relationships, never to trust another man again. And really, who could have blamed me? But no. I had been unfortunate, met a very wicked man and I would be damned if I would tar everyone with the same brush. I believe most people in this world are good, and Greg was not changing my opinion on that. If he did, I would become a bitter man-hater and that would give the power back to him. And I couldn't allow that. I had moved on, loved again, and was happy. The perfect revenge and an important message to others.

I reached over to the plate in the centre of the table and helped myself to the one remaining fortune cookie. As I broke it open, the crisp, sugary treat crumbling to display the folded piece of paper within, I couldn't help but smile as I read my fortune. "Exciting times lie ahead of you."

Like Ryan had said, who was I to doubt the wisdom of the fortune cookie?

So that was how "Playing with Fire – The true Story of Fireman Scam" was born.

22

Playing With Fire

We thought long and hard about the name for the book. Karen and I came up with so many suggestions. There were jokey titles as well as serious, hard-hitting ones. It seemed fitting that as Greg put so much of his time and effort into cultivating his character as a brave and dedicated fireman, there should be a nod to his 'profession' and the fire service. It was decided that the word 'fire' should be included in the title. A little jibe at him if you like. At his lies, his deception, his burning need to be someone he was not and would never be. It made me smile to imagine how he would react to it all; I knew the look on his face would be utterly priceless.

When our story first hit the media back in April 2020, the Daily Mail quickly ran with an article entitled "How did she fall for Fireman Scam?" The article, of course, was written to show me in a dreadful light, poke fun at me and their perceived naivety on my part. As I had expected, the vile comments had been hurtful and in their thousands. Now, nearly three years on, I was so much stronger and more determined as a person, and I found it all a little bit funny. And as *Fireman Sam* was one of Charlie's favourite cartoon heroes, I decided 'what the hell' and included it in the title too. Proving to myself and others just how far I had come and how much I had now healed.

The fictional 'James Scott' was now the brunt of our family jokes. I suppose it was a coping mechanism on our part; if we could make light of the horrible things we had been through they would no longer have any power over us. Gallows humour I suppose. We'd even had a party with fancy dress one Bank Holiday weekend, the theme being everyone was to dress as a fictional character. A close friend of ours who was always good for a laugh, came dressed as a fireman carrying a swag bag. He had even attached a prosthetic witch-like fake nose; it was a little mean and childish, I suppose, taking the piss out of Greg's conk but we couldn't help finding it hilarious. It was decided that afternoon, under the influence of a few drinks, we would have another fancy-dress party the following month and the theme would be 'Walter Mitty'. Everyone who attended got right into the spirit of it with variations on the 'James Scott' theme. One friend had even managed to obtain a costume of a penis with balls attached. It was a pale pink body stocking affair and he had even added paint and bandage to show the false bruising and dressings Greg had adorned his member with. 'Fake Vasectomy James' won the prize that afternoon. No one could top that outfit. No one even came close. It really was the dog's bollocks. Not even 'Lime Green Mankini James' stood a chance. There was much laughter from everyone that afternoon and laughter really can do you the world of good.

Karen and I completed *Playing with Fire* just in time for Christmas. We had worked tirelessly, always conscious of his release from prison coming up the following month. But we managed to complete it in good time and were happy with the final edited result. The truth was all down there in black and white. The highs, lows and every twist and turn in between. We had written the truth – the honest account of 'James Scott'. Warts and all. I was extremely proud of what we had both achieved.

Christmas Day once again arrived and was as far from the previous year as you could imagine. No longer in lockdown, hugs and kisses were in abundance. Again, the entire family descended on Scott and me and I loved every single second of it. It was so wonderful to not have all the lockdown rules and restraints, and Karen, a year on in her recovery journey, was very much back to her entertaining best self.

We all once again sat around my cramped kitchen table. It was groaning under the weight of all the festive food laid out upon it. Remnants of pulled crackers and tinsel were everywhere, glitter sparkling under the fluorescent kitchen lights. We were all fit to burst after having eaten and drank far too much as you tend to do at Christmas. Everyone was in great spirits.

Ryan tapped his fork against his nearly empty wine glass, the remnants of his red wine sloshing about in the bottom. He pushed his chair back from the table noisily and rose to his feet.

Ryan's yearly speech had now become a family tradition and a hush quickly fell over the table. He briefly cleared his throat and began speaking.

"Lovely meal once again Coleen." He raised his glass to me in a toast. "And what a special day with us all together again and enough food and booze to keep us going until the New Year."

Everyone seated around the table agreed and wine glasses were clinked together.

"And here's to Karen and Coleen." Ryan continued, his glass

still raised. "The budding authors of the family, even if they did need a kick up the arse to do it. I always knew they could do it, even when they couldn't see it themselves. Here's to *Playing with Fire.*"

"Playing with Fire," everyone chorused, their glasses raised to mirror Ryan's.

Ryan continued. "And to old 'James Walter Mitty Scott', his last Christmas in the clink, but what a welcome home gift this little paperback on his coffee table will be."

"Don't forget the podcast series," Mum interrupted, her face a little flushed from the Baileys. She wasn't usually one for drinking apart from high days and holidays. "That will be out soon too."

Mum was so proud and excited for us. Her eyes twinkling merrily, matching her festive sparkly Christmas jumper. Mum and her Christmas jumpers – another family tradition, along with her famous strawberry trifle, which didn't seem to be going anywhere.

Jon had recorded the podcast episodes with us the previous month. Travelling with Vicky Pattison to our homes over the course of a week. It was felt that if everyone was in their home settings it would make the podcast seem more natural and relaxed. That was a good call on their part.

The day Vicky came to my house I was an absolute bag of nerves. Not knowing what to expect, my stomach was in knots and my palms sweaty. But I really needn't have worried. Vicky arrived with a lovely bouquet of flowers for me and packets of sweets for Charlie. She gave me the warmest hug as soon as she walked through my front door. She was extremely glamorous but in truth she appeared as nervous as I felt. But once we started talking all my nerves melted away. As I drank my tea and Vicky sipped her water, it felt like I was having a good old natter with a close friend. I don't know what I was expecting, and I had only really ever seen Vicky on *Geordie Shore* and bits of *I'm a Celebrity... Get Me Out Of Here!* I was concerned she may be a little hard around the edges, confrontational even, but I couldn't have been more wrong. A more lovely, open, warm woman you couldn't wish to meet, and I was confident she was someone who would do justice to our story.

So, the *Love Bombed* podcast was created with a release date set for Valentine's Day. A fitting day for such a timely warning to all singletons out there. Greg was now out of prison and back walking amongst us, maybe up to all his old tricks once again.

23

Media Madness

Valentine's Day arrived, the most romantic day of the year. The shops were full of cards, plush teddies holding red love hearts and all the other assorted paraphernalia that comes along with the celebration. But for me, February 14th was completely terrifying. The previous day, at the request of Jon, I had found the courage to give some interviews about *Playing with Fire* and the podcast *Love Bombed* for the local TV and radio stations, and also on Women's Hour on BBC Radio 4. These had been nerve-wracking enough; I had barely slept a wink the nights running up to them. My anxiety levels were through the roof, but at least these interviews had been pre-recorded. Today, however, I was travelling to Manchester's Media City to appear live on BBC Breakfast alongside Chris Bentham. I was so nervous I could barely breathe. Scott was driving and as he sat alongside me, he tried his utmost to get me to calm down, reassuring me that all would be fine, but to no avail.

It was the half term school holidays, so Charlie was along for the ride too. He was totally oblivious to his mum's anxiety. He was in the back of the car holding his favourite toy – a bright orange dragon – just happy to be on an exciting road trip with his mum and dad. And with talk of taking the *Coronation Street* tour in the pipeline for the afternoon, he was more than a little excited.

The interview itself was only a few minutes long but viewed by many millions. Watching it back afterwards I couldn't deny that, despite looking like a startled deer in the headlights in my smartest black dress and boots, I had done myself proud. I managed to get my main point across, tried to show there could be light after all the darkness of deceit. That when something bad happens like what happened to our family it really is not your fault. You are the victim, you never asked for any of it, and you should never allow the person that hurt you to retain the power.

Scott gave me the biggest hug when, flustered and more than a little shaky on my feet, I had finally exited the studio.

"You were amazing Col," he beamed with evident pride and squeezed me a little tighter. "I'm so proud of my brave, strong missus." He released his grip a little to look deep into my eyes. "That can't have been easy at all, but you only bloody smashed it."

I smiled back at my husband, noticing his eyes were welling up a little. He was such a softy at heart.

"Well, all I know is that I'm glad that's finally over." I let out a relieved sigh. "Is it too early for me to have a large glass of vino?"

Charlie, at this point, was desperately tugging at my sleeve, his happy little face flushed pink with excitement. He was keen to get on with the rest of the day. See what excitement Manchester had to offer. He had already charmed the production staff with his giddiness and cheeky smile. We'd already met the guys from *The Wanted* in the Green Room, and he was eager to see what more fun there was in store.

The three of us left the studio on a high. Arm in arm with Scott and with Charlie holding on tight to my hand, I was so glad it was all over and relieved it was time to get back to a bit of normality. Little did I know that there was fat chance of that. My phone didn't stop ringing for the remainder of that day. Requests for TV and radio interviews flooded in. Everyone was staggered by our story and wanted to hear more. With trepidation I agreed to all their requests, after all this was all bound to die down soon and if I could raise some awareness that could only be a good thing. So, despite my nerves, I was going to give it a good go and get our story out there.

As expected, my BBC News interview had hit the online platforms. TikTok seems to be the one that brings out the very worst of the trolls. So, despite being pleased by how I had come across on camera there was still the mean and hurtful comments guaranteed to knock me back down. This time around though, they were definitely in the minority. Nevertheless, they were just as vile as the ones I had received back in April 2020. However, this time I felt it was more water off a duck's back. Let those nasty trolls crack on and do their worst. I was going to be the winner here. I wasn't the same person anymore. No, now I was so much more resilient.

The best thing that came out of that day was the many messages I received. Lovely, kind, encouraging words from my family and friends but also so many more from strangers. Both women and men who had seen me on their television screens that morning and wanted to reach out, share with me their stories, and some to seek advice.

My heart broke a little listening to the many stories. Some of them were truly terrible and I felt privileged that they chose me to confide it. Like me they didn't want to always be the victim and let their experience define the rest of their lives. They needed to heal, grow strong and were determined to win too. I didn't know these people, but I was proud of them all the same.

I replied to every single message, spoke to many on the phone for hours. I really hope I helped them in some way. I believe talking to someone who has been through something similar to you, but is removed from your day-to-day life, can really help you to open up. Share the pain. Take back the control. Be you once again.

24

Home Or Away

I tried not to think of Greg too much, but it wasn't easy. I just couldn't stop myself wondering what he must be feeling, seeing our story, his face everywhere. I had healed now and was strong and letting the world know who he was and what he had done. I can only imagine he was beyond livid. We were a nice, quiet middle-class family. He had foolishly believed we would not cause a fuss. That we would hide away quietly and lick our wounds, be too embarrassed to tell our story. More fool him.

Was he even still in the country to witness everything I was doing? Or had he scurried away to hide? Maybe fleeing abroad, possibly even to Germany? We knew he still kept in touch with people from his Army days. Was he still with his loyal girlfriend who would be supporting him faithfully? Had she still not wised up? The Police suspected he was still in the UK, and they were pretty sure they were still a couple.

But if they were still together, I wondered how she could reconcile herself to the knowledge of who he really was. After all, now she was bound to have seen me on the TV, heard me on the radio, had friends, family commenting on 'her' man and his many crimes.

She knew now that he had been contacting other women from prison while she was loyally visiting him and waiting patiently on the outside. Surely even she must have limits to the amount of betrayal she could stomach? She had been warned repeatedly, shown proof by me and others, and for God's sake had even witnessed Greg stand up and plead guilty to all charges in Durham Crown Court, but it seemed that her devotion to him just defied common sense.

I know Greg had considered fleeing to Germany after he had first absconded from my home. Iain had been shown text messages and Facebook messages that Greg had been sending to a woman who both Greg and Rachel had known from their time in Germany. This woman still lived there, and he was very keen to reconnect.

This woman had become wary of Greg and his persistent messages and had sent a screenshot of all the messages to Rachel, who she was still in contact with. Bizarrely, Greg was now using a fake Facebook account in the name of 'Bob Johnson'. I can only speculate as to what he was up to, having to use yet another false persona. Whatever explanation he had given this woman for his 'name change' she had initially accepted it. Reading those messages, only a few weeks after he had left me, had been heartbreaking. He was happy and flirty with this woman. No, more than flirty, he was downright sexually suggestive, hinting that they could cosy up and share a single bed together and keep each other warm. She had played along with it for a while, all the time forwarding the messages on to Rachel. Greg simply had no shame.

Back then Iain had a plan though. Get this woman totally on

side. Let Greg arrange to go to Germany, but Iain would be at Newcastle Airport as a welcoming committee, ready to confront his brother-in-law before he was able to set foot on the plane. He wanted some answers from him but also couldn't wait to see the look on his face once he realised his plans for escape had been well and truly thwarted.

It was a daft plan really. It should have been left to the Police from the start, but emotions had been running so high. Anyway, it was all to no avail. The messages from Greg to the woman in Germany suddenly stopped. Obviously, he had been tipped off about Iain's plan. Mysteriously the 'Bob Johnson' Facebook account was gone too. Who had tipped him off? I don't know. Maybe Rachel? On some level she still cared for her cheating spouse. Or had it been his new love interest in Germany? We'll never know. Maybe he still went to Germany at some point. Maybe not. But what we do know is that he was soon back in the UK and back to all his old tricks once again.

25

What A Story

The day *Playing with Fire* was finally made available for sale on Amazon, Waterstones and WH Smith's both Karen and I couldn't help but feel nervous. We really didn't expect it to receive much attention at all, but we still felt that it was 'our baby'. Something we had never previously contemplated doing but were now so proud of what we had achieved.

We had raised a glass and hugged each other, Karen joking that within a couple of months it would be languishing in the bottom of the bargain bins in the charity shops. If I'm honest though, we didn't even care, not really. Of course, we hoped it would do well, but we were realistic, never having written a book before and neither of us were recognised authors.

We felt sure that friends and family, curious neighbours and the like, would of course buy a copy and if that was all that happened, we would still be happy. We were now published authors, and no one could take that away from us.

The cover for the book had taken us quite some time to decide upon. We had first considered an impressive five tier wedding cake with a little fireman topper standing alongside his bride. Greg had been adamant that we had to have a 'fireman' themed cake. The lower tiers would be adorned with different things representing his lies and deceit.

I had initially liked this idea and we even got a cover image mocked up and had asked family and friends for their opinions too. Their responses, on the whole, were very positive but I still wasn't completely sure. I felt in my heart it would make our book appear to would-be readers as a rom com and not the true-life story of manipulation and fraud that it really was.

"It seems a little flippant," I commented to Karen as I held the illustration in my hand, carefully studying it. "Don't you agree? I feel it needs to be more raw, stripped back to the bones of my relationship with Greg. Just a simple picture of him and me together, appearing to any onlookers as just another happy couple, deeply in love. Me completely oblivious as to what the truth really was and what was to come."

Karen had agreed. "I think, you're right, but would you be ok with your photo being out there, you and him together?"

I shrugged. "It makes no difference to me now."

The media had already released so many pictures over the years, what did one more really matter? And for once, this one I got to choose. I just felt this would make for a better cover. Help the reader connect more with the story.

Karen had been in full agreement. "You're definitely right Col, but what picture do you want to go with?"

That, I was not so sure of. I hated having to sit down and sift through the many pictures of Greg and me. Smiling, happy images of a life that never really existed. It made me sick to my stomach, but it was a means to an end. So finally, after a long afternoon of deliberating, Karen and I came to a final decision.

"This is the one," I announced triumphantly, just happy the task was over with.

It was a full-length image of me and 'James'. We had been out at an animal farm with Charlie. It was a cold autumnal day, and we were dressed warmly for the chilly weather, in thick winter coats and woolly scarves. Karen and Ryan had been with us that day too. It had been a lovely day, overall. The only upset had been when we had all heard Greg receive a call from his consultant regarding his ongoing treatment for his testicular cancer.

We had all stood silently, our happy chatter gone, as we waited patiently with bated breath for any news. All of us could clearly hear the male voice of the doctor on the other end of the phone. Who was that man? There was no cancer , no doctor. Greg had got someone to pretend to be his consultant. Why would they have agreed to that? Yes, this picture would be perfect for the cover. It would always remind me of that family day out and the despicable lengths to which that man could stoop.

The decision was made. The book was on sale and one of the first copies bought was my very own. I wanted it proudly there on my coffee table for all the world to see. To make me smile when I walked past and caught a glimpse of it, or when I resolutely put my mug of tea down firmly on his smug face. It gave me a little kick every time I did that. Silly really, but it was just another small way to show I had not been beaten by that man.

26

Runaway Success

The sales for the book were, as we had initially expected, mostly family and friends. Nice reviews were left, with kind words. However, day by day we started to see the sales steadily increase. Possibly from people listening to the *Love Bombed* podcast, eager to learn more about our story. Or perhaps it was word of mouth? Whatever the reason, Karen and I were elated.

We sold more copies of the book that first week than we had honestly expected to sell in total. People were even purchasing it overseas. It was funny to think of our words being read in the USA, Germany, Spain, and as far away as Australia. The feedback we were receiving from the reviews was overall very positive. As expected, it's impossible to please everyone, but the majority of the reviewers really enjoyed it. One review did leave me speechless. The reader had enjoyed the book, however had admitted to feeling disappointed that there was not more violence in it. In his words he much preferred a true story with "more blood and guts". I was sorry he hadn't enjoyed it but not sorry about the lack of gory bits. It's just not that type of story.

It's about love bombing, coercion, manipulation. In fact, a love story that just went very, very wrong.

After finishing reading, both women and men had reached out to me and Karen directly. This had happened previously, firstly after my television and radio appearances and then when the podcast had been released. Far more people got in touch after reading the book though. Perhaps they felt they knew us so much better now, had connected with us as a family. They were keen to wish us luck and for us all to be happy. Others wanted to share their own experiences and to let us know we were all in this together.

I was completely staggered by just how similar some of the stories I was being told were to ours. I began to realise that the behaviour of 'James' was not actually unique. Maybe the lengths he went to were unusually elaborate but there were sadly many, many other 'James' characters out there.

The problem is too many people are ashamed to speak out, to report it to the police and try to get justice. Society is very quick to cast judgement on the victim, to point out their failings, but they have all the facts after the event, plus the luxury of hindsight. They did not love that person, they were not being controlled. Society needs to take a step back, look at the bigger picture and just be a little bit kinder.

I was so happy that our words were helping others. Of course, it would be fantastic if *Playing with Fire* did well, made us some money, go some way to recouping some of the money Karen had lost. The £1,000 a month Greg was court-ordered to pay was sporadic to say the least.

We'd expected him to renege on payments once he was released from prison on licence and that was exactly what he was doing.

So even though Karen could do with making some money, that had never been our driving force. With that thought in the forefront of our minds we both decided we would like to donate a percentage from all our book sales to Women's Aid – a charity working against domestic abuse, striving to keep women and children safe. Our money could really make a difference. The tale of Greg Wilson's crimes actually helping others – it just seemed fitting. It will go some way to righting the wrongs.

27

If Only

Karen and I were so happy. The book was doing better than we ever could have anticipated. The *Love Bombed* podcast also receiving amazing feedback. Hitting the number 1 position in the Apple chart downloads in its very first week.

I was still being approached by other victims. Some were tentatively reaching out for a bit of help and advice, others just wanted someone to listen to their story. Someone who had been through something similar and would understand and not ridicule.

One lady wasn't a stranger to me. I knew her and she knew Greg. Back in 2016 we would see her regularly. She was called Casey. She had worked on the reception at Ramside Spa and I would often see her whilst visiting the gym on a morning before work. Back then I was desperately trying to shift the last few pounds of stubborn baby weight, to fit into my beautiful, extremely tight-fitted wedding dress. It was hanging proudly on the door of my wardrobe, all ready to go and mocking me every time I walked past. It silently chastised me for the Chinese takeaway or tube of Pringles I had scoffed. Despite worries about the zip bursting on the dress, I was excited for the day I would finally wear it. What a waste of time all that effort was. Greg must have been having a good old laugh at my expense, knowing all my efforts would be in vain. There was never going to be a wedding, the beautiful dress never to be worn – at least not by me. All those wasted mornings when I could have caught up on an extra hour of much-needed sleep rather than huffing and puffing, red faced and sweaty, on the rowing machine.

We were often to be seen at the Ramside spa and gym, as Greg was buying a grand house that overlooked the golf course on the prestigious Ramside Estate. The purchase of the house boasted four memberships to use the gymnasium, spa and Golf Club. All of the amenities in the leisure suite were simply amazing. These lifetime membership passes would cost hundreds of pounds a month. The fact that these passes were issued to us before contracts had exchanged, the keys to the property handed over, just showed the amount of sway Greg had over people.

Greg was letting everyone believe he was purchasing the grand, palatial house on the Ramside Estate. He was conning everyone that he had the funds and the means for such an extravagant purchase. It wasn't just myself and my family that were hoodwinked by him. It was also Estate Agents, Solicitors, builders, interior designers and the like. They all believed every word that Greg fed them. Right to the point that contracts were drawn up, ready to exchange. Everything on the final snagging list had been ticked off and everyone was champing at the bit to complete. No one knew that Greg never had the slightest intention of actually purchasing the property. How could he? He was skint, after all.

The money defrauded from Karen was never going to last

that long, not when you were leading the life that Greg enjoyed. However, his dedication to his 'craft' fooled everyone. His carefully constructed documents – all fraudulent forgeries, but so convincing that astute businessmen, experts in their own fields, never doubted him for a second. They too swept up in all his lies.

I would often chat to Casey whilst visiting the gym on a morning before work. I can remember her being a lovely girl; very pretty with an open, warm demeanour. Any time I would go in with Charlie she would always make a great fuss of him. He would smile and giggle in delight when he saw her.

She had just finished listening to the podcast and had felt the need to reach out to me. She had things she felt I needed to know. Firstly, how much she had enjoyed *Love Bombed*, but more importantly what she herself knew about Greg. Casey, you see, had known Greg long before I did. Sometime before starting her job at Ramside Hall she had been employed by House of Fraser in the centre of Darlington – the town where Greg lived with his wife and three boys. She remembered Greg coming into the store, hand in hand with Rachel. He would often stop and while away some time chatting with Casey while Rachel was busy shopping. Let's face it, Greg always did love a pretty face.

Casey had been delighted when she had first spotted Greg at her reception desk. It was always nice to reconnect with a friendly face from the past. She had greeted him warmly and said how lovely it was to see him after such a long time. He had instantly cut the conversation dead, claiming that it was purely a case of mistaken identity and they had never met before. He even made a joke about how he must have had a doppelganger, but it certainly couldn't have been him shopping in House of

Fraser with his wife.

She had gone on to tell me that she had felt embarrassed. She must have made a mistake. Greg wasn't the man she had chatted to all those times before. But she knew in her heart she wasn't wrong. And what she couldn't deny was the sheepish look on his face like he'd been caught with his hand in the cookie jar. Although I hadn't been in earshot of this conversation, Casey wondered to herself if she had inadvertently dropped Greg in it somehow.

She had tried to push Greg a little further, telling herself that he had just forgotten her and she would need to jog his memory. She remembered recalling an occasion when he was shopping with his wife. Rachel had been desperate to buy a leather jacket they stocked; she had fallen in love with it but was hoping to get it at a discounted price. So, they had come into the store every time there was a discounted event on, hoping to bag themselves a bargain. Casey had asked Greg if Rachel ever managed to get that jacket. He had become extremely flustered, anxiously looking around to check I was out of earshot. He had beads of sweat filming on his brow. He, again, adamantly denied ever having met Casey before, telling her it was most definitely a case of mistaken identity. It wasn't him and they had never met. He was so insistent that she had finally agreed that she must have been wrong. But it never sat well with her. She knew in her heart it had definitely been him, so why on earth was he lying? It made no sense.

Casey had spoken to me many times at the reception desk, and she knew I was aware that he had been married before. She was bewildered by his reaction, and it had left her feeling extremely uneasy. What Casey hadn't known, of course, was that I believed Greg was divorced from a lady called Gill, and they had two daughters. Not a woman called Rachel with three sons. And after all 'Gill' lived in the USA and would not be likely to be traipsing around House of Fraser in Darlington trying to obtain a discounted leather jacket.

After that encounter he had always been extra friendly to her whenever he had come to the spa. Casey thought maybe he felt bad for being so abrupt with her when they had talked previously. For cutting her off and disregarding what she had been saying. With hindsight it was more likely he was trying to keep her sweet and avoid any chance of her speaking to me alone.

He would chat to Casey about his many business interests and plans. Taking her number, promising to let her know of any business opportunities he could involve her in. She would tell me that he would text her quite often, promising upcoming interviews that would never transpire, great job opportunities that never seemed to come to anything. Even suggesting that she come work for him in his new business venture in Newcastle – the old nightclub Pravda on the Quayside that he was in the process of converting into a restaurant and nightclub. She forwarded me a screenshot of his contract details that were still saved in her phone. She had him logged 'James Scott – Newcastle Hotel'. She even had a little emoji of a money bag next to his name, because she too, like everyone else, was convinced of his wealth.

Of course, there never was a job for Casey. Even though, by that point she believed he was who he purported to be she couldn't shake off the niggling feeling of unease. She was good with faces and though Greg was adamant he wasn't the shopper from House of Fraser, she knew without a shadow of a doubt that he was lying.

It was shortly after this that Casey noted we suddenly stopped attending the spa and she had no further contact with Greg. Over the years that followed she would sometimes think about him and wonder what the truth really was. She just had a bad feeling about the man and what he had been up to. Casey was obviously a very good judge of character.

28

Despicable Deceptions

I was pleased that Casey had got in touch. She was obviously annoyed with herself for not having said something all those years earlier when she felt something wasn't quite right with Greg's behaviour. But in all honesty, what could she have really said? Hindsight is a wonderful thing. Yes, she'd had a bad feeling about the man, but truthfully it was none of her business. And even if she had brought the subject back up with Greg, or mentioned it to me, he would have just brushed it aside, he was so good at covering his tracks. He'd had a lot of practice at it. No doubt he would have already had a completely feasible explanation ready to go if needed, to shut the topic down, to convince me that Casey was just mistaken. Greg would never have risked us having any sort of conversation that could risk his life and lies being exposed.

If the name Rachel had been mentioned, the game would have been well and truly up for him. If I had found out the truth back then he would have been out on his ear. Casey had seen him out and about with Rachel. Thinking back, this would have been around the time he decided to accompany me on all my morning trips to the gym. Which meant we also had to bring a sleepy, grumpy Charlie along too, despite my protestations that I was fine and could easily make my own way there. He had insisted. He would just have a nice coffee and bacon butty, he assured me, and wait for me in the bar area. It was no trouble at all, he said. He must have been on tenterhooks the whole time I visited the gym, ready to swoop in if anything was mentioned. If it became clear that Casey and I were chatting about anything more than the weather, Charlie, or my dislike for the treadmill. But as the case always seemed to be with Greg, he needn't have worried.

After listening to the whole of the podcast series Casey not only felt a little sad for not having trusted her gut instincts about Greg all those years before, but she also felt disgusted. Disgusted that the man had lied about having cancer. Using this lie for his own selfish benefit. As a way to keep his lies going, gaining sympathy and support, revelling in it when there was absolutely nothing wrong with his health.

She told me that she had, in fact, had cancer since we had last seen her. At only 25 she had been shocked to be diagnosed with cervical cancer and had to undergo radical surgery and treatment. Bravely she had decided to speak up about her story and raise awareness of the importance of young women going for their smear tests. She had done interviews and appeared in newspapers. She even undertook a charity sky dive in aid of Jo's Cervical Cancer Trust. After Casey contacted me, I read all the articles and interviews she had given. I was in awe of her bravery and resilience. It seemed that she, too, wanted to make some good come out of a horrible experience.

It made me so angry to hear her story, once again hitting home just how wicked it is to lie about having cancer. But it had been a means to an end for Greg. He had so easily played the cancer card when in reality there were so many ordinary people fighting the cruel disease.

A few days later I saw Karen at her house in Chester-Le-Street and told her all I had discovered from Casey. Karen's battle with cancer was still being fought bravely each day, but the reminder of the care and sympathy we had all given to him, along with his mum's fake cancer diagnosis, was too much for her to hear again. Cancer had never been Greg's fight. It had been Casey's, and it had been hers.

29

Karen

Karen's face looked so sad, as if she was on the verge of imminent tears.

I felt concern for my sister rise up in me and rubbed her arm gently. "Are you OK sis?"

She shook her head forcefully. "It's just makes me sad to hear about another person in the club that nobody ever wants to be a member of. The 'Big C Club'.

I nodded at my sister, understanding only too well what she meant. I had seen what she had endured over the past few years. I knew she was still emotionally bruised from her two cancer diagnoses, and the surgeries and treatments that were still ongoing. How could she not be? Even if things seemed a lot brighter for her health-wise, there was always that lingering worry that the horrible disease would be back. Every ache and pain taking on a sinister edge. The build up to every CT scan, the horrible 'scanxiety' that accompanied it. It was a dark cloud to live under.

I felt so angry at Greg on my sister's behalf. "It just makes me so mad that Greg used cancer to garner sympathy from people and to enable him to carry on his deceit." Anger bubbled up in me just thinking about him again. "Everyone in life is touched by cancer in one way or another – either themselves or someone they love. For him to use a fake diagnosis is just so sick."

My sister nodded her head again. "It is, but then he's just thoroughly rancid through and through. I bet it never gave him a single second's thought about how much bad taste it was all in. He won't have lost a wink of sleep over it, I know that much."

Karen, clearly very upset, rose from her seat and headed to her kitchen to put the kettle on to make us both a cup of tea. Sometimes it just seemed the best thing to do. I doubted a cup of tea would make anything better, but it certainly wouldn't make things any worse. It was just a very British thing to do. I heard her rummaging around in the kitchen cupboards, I suspected she was trying to locate some decent biscuits to cheer us up. Bugger the calories there was bigger things to worry about.

Five minutes later we were sitting, once again, nursing our mugs of strong tea and devouring the fancy biscuits.

Karen looked thoughtful. "You know the thing is though? A lot of good has come out of the bad when you think about it."

I blew on my tea to cool it. "How so?"

Karen went on to explain exactly what she meant. Through-out her life she had always harboured a little dream of writing. As a child at Primary school, she had written amazing stories about faraway lands where her teddy bears could play and would spend much of her spare time lost in this magical world of her own creation. I could clearly remember her as a little girl with a notebook in hand, scribbling down page after page. However, as she grew older and peer pressure kicked in, she realised this was not the norm. Her friends were playing with Barbie dolls and listening to *Bucks Fizz*, not spending their evenings, sitting in their bedrooms, writing.

She sadly put her notebook away and there it stayed for many decades, her dreams along with it. Life was busy and during the years that followed, there was always something more important to do than return to her love of writing. She would often think back wistfully to her writing days and wished it was something she could have pursued. But sadly she didn't have the confidence to do it.

My sister had always been an avid reader, but she had dreamed that in another life someone would actually be able to read her words.

Life after Greg was desperately grim for my twin. She had lost her career, her properties, had been forced into inevitable bankruptcy and then, to add the icing to a very unpalatable cake, she had gone on to be diagnosed with not one but two cancers in quick succession.

Having lost everything and fearing she would also lose her life, Karen had been understandably in a very dark place for many months. She had always been the 'funny' one in the family. The one that would make everyone burst into spontaneous laughter with her dry, sometimes crude wit. Often our mum would be wiping the tears of laughter from her eyes, declaring, "Karen you're terrible, I don't know where you get it from, it's certainly not my side of the family".

She had always been the one that kept our spirits high. But her spirit had been well and truly crushed. I hated to see it.

And then we had written *Playing with Fire.* It was a chance for me and Karen to finally write and, although she had been nervous initially, she thoroughly enjoyed the process. OK, the subject matter was tough at times, but just to be able to sit at her dining room table and let the words flow was so good for her soul. It was cathartic for us both.

After writing our memoir together she went on to write a work of fiction – something she'd dreamed of doing for many decades. It is an uplifting tale of a woman who gets knocked down flat on her arse by life and has to get up, dust herself off and grab life by the dangly bits. Not unlike Karen's own story. They always do say write about what you know.

The Reinvention of Lottie Potts is a funny, feel-good story that can't help but bring a smile to the gloomiest of faces. It has plenty of naughty humour in it too – that is just so 'my sister'.

Like *Playing with Fire*, Karen wanted her novel to do some good in the world. To create a bit of a legacy for herself. So, she decided to donate a portion of all sales to Epilepsy Society and Great Ormond Street Hospital. Charities that are incredibly close to her heart as her little grandson suffers with drug resistant Epilepsy and often travels to London, to Great Ormond Street Hospital, and the truly amazing staff do incredible work.

As Karen had always said: "Never give up on yourself no matter how far you fall. Just stick with it as there's a plan for your life, a pattern, and it may not make sense when you are in the depths of despair, but just keep on keeping on. At some point in the future things will improve and everything will begin to make sense, just as long as you never give up."

A mantra that my twin sister and I both live by, and one that has kept us strong throughout the last few difficult years.

30

The Bigger Picture

Karen and I were still reeling at the buzz around the podcast and our book's release. As sales steadily increased our confidence had grown too. Together we had produced something that was helping others. The more our story got out there, the more interest it sparked. And one Monday afternoon I was in for yet another surprise. I was just sitting minding my own business in the doctors' surgery waiting room, flicking through an out-of-date *Woman's Own* and reading a fascinating article about ten things to do with left over Christmas pudding. Not terribly helpful when you're at the back end of a frosty February. I was just having a bit of a check-up but was desperately trying to keep myself calm as I knew a blood pressure check would be in the offing. I now suffered terribly from 'white coat syndrome'. My blood pressure reading at home would be in the normal range, but any medical environment would send it soaring. So, this visit to the doctor was guaranteed to make it shoot up. I often wondered if this was connected to my previous experiences of hospital. The trauma of nearly losing Charlie, maybe a little PTSD. Whatever the reason, I was trying my level best to keep calm.

My phone was on silent and vibrated in my leather handbag on the back of my chair. As my appointment wasn't for another ten minutes, I opened it my bag and fumbled around desperately to locate the device amongst the used tissues and random items that defined my life. Did I really need to carry around bits of old Lego and four different shades of lipstick? I was keen to discover who had messaged. It was, in fact, a Facebook Messenger message from a woman's name I did not recognise. I quickly scrolled down the lengthy message, shocked by its content. This woman worked for a media company and had been commissioned to produce a documentary – and she would very much like our story to be part of it.

The documentary was to be told from the victim's point of view and how we had eventually got justice. Suffice to say my blood pressure was well and truly through the roof at that point. I didn't know how I felt. I could, of course, see the benefits of agreeing to her request. It was another opportunity to tell our story. Isn't that what we had always wanted to do? But this was on a different level – it would be aired on prime-time TV on one of the major channels. Was I really ready for that? I could feel the nerves already beginning to kick in. This was well and truly out of my comfort zone.

Once home I called Karen to ask her opinion and, as always, she was all for it. She could see the potential; she thought it was a fantastic opportunity.

"It'll be great Coleen," she reasoned with me, obviously trying to silence my doubts. "It's going to be our words, more publicity and more help for Women's Aid. Think about it sis, it's a complete no-brainer."

The rest of the family agreed with Karen. We all got together a few days later for Sunday lunch at *Fabio's* in Chester-Le-Street – a local Italian restaurant near to Karen and Ryan's house that did a mean spaghetti Bolognese at a very reasonable price. As it was Sunday though, their Sunday lunch menu was also on offer. Karen and I had to give them credit, as Yorkshire lasses we couldn't fault their Yorkshire puds – they were really delicious.

The main topic of conversation was, of course, the suggested documentary.

Ryan pushed his Yorkshire pudding onto Karen's plate. As a South African he had never got his head around the point of a good old Yorkie. Karen wasn't complaining, every time they went out for a roast dinner, she always got an extra portion.

"I don't mind being in the documentary if they want me," Ryan said. "Mind you, I don't know if the world is ready for my ugly mug in high definition."

Karen jumped in loyally to support him. "Rubbish! You'd give Chris Hemsworth a right run for his money in the looks department." Chris was Karen's celebrity crush.

I couldn't help but snort at this. Everyone turned to hear where the unattractive noise had emanated from. "Chris Hemsworth? Do me a favour. More like Chris Moyles, you mean?"

Scott laughed at this. He loved a bit of "Moylsey" on Radio X in the morning. "Cheer up fella, at least he's got the gift of the gab."

So, it was decided that afternoon over a lovely three course lunch with plenty of wine, that we would inform the production company first thing on Monday morning that we were 'all in' with the documentary.

Over the course of the next few months, a further three media companies got in touch, all keen to make a documentary of their own. Our story was definitely in demand. So, what the Hell? In for a penny, in for a pound.

31

More To Give

Whilst the first documentary was well under way the book was still gaining momentum. I was invited to appear on *This Morning* on ITV. Despite my nerves jangling, I decided to push myself. I was more than aware how many people tuned into the show every morning and therefore knew that if I didn't grasp this opportunity, I would definitely regret it.

This was a platform to promote the book, get the story out to so many people, and ultimately help Women's Aid.

Karen, too, had been invited to sit on the famous sofa with me and speak to Holly Willoughby and Phillip Schofield. That helped to relieve some of my nerves, knowing I wasn't going to have to do it alone. Sadly, however, Karen didn't get to appear with me. We travelled down to London together on the train the day before and she had every intention of supporting me. But the long journey and the hustle and bustle of London proved just too much for her. She was doing very well on her cancer recovery journey but could sometimes push herself a little too far and then the inevitable exhaustion would take hold.

I couldn't help but feel a little guilty. Should I have just gone on my own? But Karen being Karen would not hear a word of it.

"Don't be daft," she laughed. "I feel like I'm the one letting you down, you having to do this on your own again. The least I can do is be here with you for moral support, even if it takes me a few days to recover."

This had made me smile. Karen was headstrong, but she was right. We were quite a team. Quite a family.

Karen may not have been up to sitting on the famous sofa opposite Phil and Holly that morning, but she was only a matter of a few feet away. She stood off to one side, just out of vision of the cameras, trying her best not to trip over the equipment. Knowing she was there, rooting for me, made it so much easier. A real comfort.

I still felt a little bit like a deer caught in the headlights during the interview but tried to answer all the questions put to me as calmly as I could. Phil even held up a copy of our book and gave it a little plug at the end of the interview.

Thanks to this, during the course of that day, the book sales soared. The support for us was amazing and heartwarming. It really touched us deeply. So many people wanted to know what had gone on to happen in our lives next. How was Charlie now, was he happy? Was I settled and had I found happiness? How was Karen's health and had she got any of her money back? Had Greg ever reformed? People were so keen to know if there was much more to come in our story.

Karen and I had never for a second anticipated people taking so much interest in our little lives. They were really invested in us as a family. Wishing the very best for us. Eager to know we were all doing well, and our lives had improved. Our book *Playing with Fire* had ended on a question. A cliff hanger I suppose. We know Greg had been contacting other women, lying and cheating right up to his sentencing day, but had he repented in prison? Had he become a better man on his release? Maybe there was much more of a story to be told.

As we sat in the back of the car to start the long journey home from London, I scrolled through all the different messages pinging through on my phone. I showed Karen just how many I was receiving, and all the questions I was being asked.

After scanning them, taking in the general gist of the comments, she looked at me with a small smile on her face. "You know what Col? Let's write a second book."

32

Healing From The Burns

"What about *After Burn*?" Karen suggested. "That kind of sums up our story – what happened after we were so burnt. *Playing with Fire* was the start, now our next story is how we recovered and rose from the ashes of it all."

I thought for a few seconds, weighing up the pros and cons in my mind, but then shook my head. "Nope, I don't agree. I don't think you can compare what he did to us as something you just slap a bit of Aloe Vera on and hope for the best. The title really needs to encapsulate our recovery process."

We had been sitting in my living room for several hours trying to decide on a name for our follow up book and were not having much luck. Many names had been quickly suggested and just as quickly disregarded. I was conscious that the day was soon coming to an end. And I would need to be sorting out everyone's teas. The kids would soon be charging through the front door, dropping bags and muddy shoes everywhere, and complaining they were starving.

Karen thought for a few seconds. "Surely recovery is healing too? Not just physical healing but healing from the mental anguish as well?"

I watched my sister take a sip of her coffee. That must have been at least her fifth of the afternoon. She had come to visit for a few days and, as always, I was over the moon to see her. I probably should have been serving decaffeinated coffee, the amount we had already got through. We would never sleep tonight at this rate.

I agreed with what Karen said though. Healing was a good word and I strongly believed that as a family we had all healed really well. Of course, and to be expected, we still encountered the odd knock back along the way, but we'd done pretty well overall and were all in a much better place.

"Why don't we simply call it *Healing from the burns* then?" I suggested, picking up my empty coffee cup ready to head into the kitchen to put the kettle on once again. I put the cup down on the coffee table, deciding I still had more to say. "We all played with fire, got burnt, but good has followed bad and we have all healed. We still are healing, probably. Always will be in one way or another."

Karen smiled back. "I like it. It's the truth. We are healing but I think the scars will always be there to some degree."

"Well," she announced, holding her now empty coffee cup in the air. "I now pronounce our second book well and truly in the pipeline."

"Hear, hear," I echoed. "*Healing from the burns.* May all who read it, enjoy it, and hopefully gain some strength from it as well." I sighed heavily. "Just one thing I think you're forgetting. We still need to write it and that's not going to be an easy task. We've got a long way still to go."

"Nonsense," Karen scoffed, batting my doubts aside.

"There's much more to be told and that's what we are going to do. Anyway, a story as odd as the 'James Scott' farce will pretty much write itself. It really is true that sometimes fact is stranger than fiction."

So that was that. It had been decided and Karen and I went back to the basics. We started a timeline as we had done with *Playing with Fire*. We were both mindful that this book would be very different from its predecessor. This time we were telling our story but we were no longer in the dark with Greg pulling all of our strings. We were now well and truly in the light and armed with all the facts. We were dealing with the devastating aftermath that man had left. But it was a good story. It wasn't all doom and gloom because it had hope and positivity in there too. And my family being the characters they all are, there would be a fair few laughs along the way.

33

Like A Bad Smell

Karen and I were invited to appear on Channel 4's *Steph's Packed Lunch* to talk to Steph McGovern about *Playing with Fire*, along with the work on our new book *Healing from the burns*. We were told that our appearance would also be used to raise awareness of romance fraud which is on the up and becoming more of a problem in wider society, especially since lockdown. Sadly, again I ended up doing the interview on my own. Karen and Ryan came along to support me but Karen wasn't physically up to doing the interview.

We had set off to the studios at the crack of dawn on that Friday morning. I was smartly dressed in a knitted black dress with gold buttons and long boots. I felt I looked smart enough. I was nervous but excited too. As the studio was in Leeds, we had decided to go for a few drinks afterwards before returning home. Hailing from Leeds ourselves, Karen and I were keen to rediscover some of our old haunts and see how much things had changed in the many years since we had last lived there.

I was scheduled to speak for six minutes or so, but the producer ended up deciding to let my interview overrun to nearly ten minutes in total. After I had opened up and started telling our story, there really was no stopping me. When the interview concluded, Steph and the crew all gave me warm hugs and this calmed my anxiety down and made me confident that I had done ok.

I had spoken about what had happened to us from my heart and how other victims were not to blame, that there was help and understanding out there. I spoke also about victim shaming and how unacceptable and damaging this could be.

The studio audience were lovely too. They were so supportive and kind – one lady even reached out to me with her contact details because she was an advocate for women, empowering them and was eager to join up with me so we could work together in supporting others.

By the time I had returned to the green room I was feeling quite overwhelmed, but Karen and Ryan were there eagerly waiting my return. Scott had also wanted to come but my priority was to keep things as normal as possible at home for Charlie. I had left Scott in charge of packed lunches and the school run that day. But I knew without a shadow of a doubt my hubby would be at home watching me live on TV, cheering me on from many miles away.

On entering the green room, Karen jumped up from her seat and ran the few steps over to me to envelop me in a massive hug.

"You were amazing Col. Ryan and I have been sitting here watching you with tears in our eyes. Your words were so strong and powerful."

I hugged my sister back, happy it was all over and with the hope that my blood pressure could now return so some sort of normal level.

"You know what you didn't do though?"

I looked at my sister, "What didn't I do?"

She laughed at me. "You forgot to mention our book. That was the whole reason you were doing the interview – to promote the flipping book and to let people know we were also writing a follow up."

"Shit!" The expletive was out of my mouth before I could stop myself. I cast my mind back over the interview. "Surely I must have mentioned it somewhere?"

But no, Karen was right. I'd been so engrossed talking about positivity, how bad victim shaming could be and how happiness was the best revenge, that I'd totally forgotten to mention the name of our book. I'd mentioned the book, I just hadn't said what it was called.

"I'm so sorry." I looked at my sister to gauge her mood, and was relieved to see she was smiling. I couldn't help but start to laugh.

"What's so funny?" Ryan looked puzzled.

"Well, no one can accuse me of being pushy, I suppose. I get invited on to the show to plug our book and, silly sod that I am, I forget to even mention its name."

Ryan laughed along with me. "It was like someone had put a couple of Duracell batteries in you. Once you started talking you couldn't stop. Poor Steph could hardly get a word in edgeways."

But whatever I had said that day had certainly done the trick. Once again people reached out. I still got some negative comments – that was to be expected. But I had learnt that those were just par for the course. I've come to understand that people who need to make fun or be cruel deserve our indifference. Imagine if the only way you could feel happy was by taunting or abusing victims – what a miserable existence that must be.

Once back at home I shared the interview to my Facebook page. I was keen for all my friends to see it. One comment I received from a friend answered some questions that I had. It was from Greg's auntie-in-law.

"We've just seen the Muppet in Durham," the message said.

I couldn't help laughing. Muppet was such an apt way of describing Greg and showed what level of regard his former family held him in.

I privately messaged her back, keen to discover more. It was, in fact, her son that had seen him in Durham City Centre only a few miles away from Chester-Le-Street. Large as life and apparently twice as ugly. He was wearing what she described as 'tree surgeon-like attire'. Was he now a gardener or something similar? Whatever he was up to it appeared he was now gainfully employed by someone. However, you never knew with Greg. Maybe a tree surgeon was his new persona. Perhaps he figured it would be a guaranteed knicker dropper for the ladies. I doubted, however, whether it would ever be quite on par with fireman.

Greg and his cousin-in-law had locked eyes. There was no love lost between the two of them as Greg's lies had impacted the whole of their family too. Had left repercussions that would not be forgotten any time soon. Greg's face, I was told, was an absolute picture as he 'shit himself' and scurried away like a scalded cat. That was one question I had always wondered now answered. Greg hadn't left the country or moved away from the North East but had chosen to stay close to his crimes. Apparently he was working, but he still wasn't paying his debts. The money owed to me from the Court judgement was paid infrequently and often not the amount specified by the Court.

It was clear that he only made payment when he feared that he would be inevitably dragged back into Court as he was still on licence for the remainder of his sentence.

I hated to think of him still living so close to my family. Why had he stayed? Surely he must have burnt all of his bridges. Was he still with his girlfriend after all this time? Had she stuck with him as we all suspected? It was unbelievable to us that they could still be together after the truth was out there, but maybe we would never know. I hoped someday I would have an answer.

34

A Leopard Doesn't Change Its Spots

It was a chilly winter evening at 7.32pm when I would get my answer to those very questions.

After tucking Charlie into bed for the night I'd taken myself off to bed early to watch a bit of television. I fancied a little easy watching escapism to de-stress. Maybe a bit of *Gavin & Stacey* or something else I had watched a gazillion times. It had been a pretty stressful day already; I'd been sent a raw draft copy the documentary that had been filmed earlier that month, to fact check and provide my feedback on it. This was the second documentary I had now had the opportunity to watch, and both were due to be aired in 2024. Watching my life unfold on the big screen didn't get any easier. I hated seeing myself in all my glory, hearing my voice. I had never been the most confident of people and this was seriously out of my comfort zone. But it needed to be done.

Karen had also watched parts of both drafts of the documentaries. She had managed to make it through about ten minutes each time before throwing in the towel. She said she couldn't bear to see herself on screen. She knew the camera put on ten pounds but had laughingly joked she didn't realise it gave you four chins too. As most women do, we like a flattering camera angle and this most definitely wasn't that. It seemed like we had been filmed from the floor upwards. Karen joked that when the documentaries aired, she would be leaving the country.

I was now happily engrossed in the drama unfolding on *Coronation Street* when my phone pinged on the pillow next to me. It was a message request on Instagram from a woman's name I did not recognise. I picked it up and squinted at the screen, thinking it was probably someone who had read *Playing with Fire.* I clicked the button to accept the request. The question that came through was a million miles away from what I had expected.

It was Greg's girlfriend's Auntie, and she wanted my help. She apologised for contacting me after everything I had been through but was at a loss as to what else she could do. Her niece was very much still in a relationship with Greg. She had stood by him the whole time he was in prison and now he was released, they were living together not too far away from where he had lived with me. The time that Greg and I had been together now, in some ways, seemed a million years ago but also like yesterday.

I finally had the answer to the questions we had all been wondering over the years. We knew she had been there supporting him in court. She even had been rude to my family, but I hoped after everything in the media, she would have wised up. Seemingly not.

Her Auntie was distraught. The messages I went on to receive detailed her family's worries. Greg had her niece well and truly under his narcissistic spell. Subsequently this had caused her relationship with her Auntie and her own mother to become practically non-existent. They were heartbroken and wanted their niece and daughter back. But sadly she had repeatedly chosen Greg over her own family. They all wanted her to end the relationship with him when they learnt the truth of who he actually was, but she was having none of it.

Greg's girlfriend's mum had read *Playing with Fire* and was desperate to know if the woman who featured at the end of the book was her daughter. The woman who had contacted me on the day of his sentencing, telling me about her relationship with Greg, or was it in fact someone else? Because this would prove, beyond doubt, that he had not changed his cheating ways. And she hoped it would be a way to get him out of all of their lives forever.

I couldn't help but still be a little shocked that his young girlfriend had stuck with him. I knew the police still believed they were together. I guess, deep down, I always knew they were too, but just didn't want to accept it. I'd hoped she had seen the light and got away from him. But I knew better than anyone how manipulative the man could be. She had been given all the facts – by me, the media and even the Crown Court – a luxury I never had. And she still chose to believe him.

My naïve hope that Greg had reformed in prison, become a better person, had already collapsed when we applied for Charlie's adoption. That hope was now well and truly trampled into the dirt. These messages I was now receiving detailed how they were convinced he was cheating on her niece and had probably been with many other women.

I forwarded her the message I received on sentencing day, from the woman he was supposedly taking to Dubai, proving this wasn't from her niece, and he was still lying and cheating. I really hoped it would do some good; unequivocally prove the low-life he really was. But as we continued to converse through messages, I sincerely doubted it. It seemed he really had got this poor girl, who was obviously so besotted by him, believing everything he told her. Quite clearly, she swallowed every bit of rubbish she was fed.

When Greg had finally been arrested it had been from the house he was living in with this girlfriend. She witnessed Chris Bentham take her man away in handcuffs. She even attended the police station in the following days to give a bad character reference about Greg and his crimes to Chris. The very same police officer who had arrested Greg in front of her.

Within a couple of days, she had decided to retract her statement. According to her Auntie she now claimed that Chris Bentham was not in fact a real police officer, but a man masquerading as one. Greg had convinced her of this and that everything said against him was malicious lies. My family had a grudge and were out to ruin him and Chris was helping. Poor Greg was the real victim!

35

All In It Together

I was at a loss about what else I could do to help this poor family. "My door is always open to you, and I will help in any way I can," I had messaged. I didn't want to blame her niece, as I knew in my heart she was a victim too, but realistically if she was going to believe that Chris was a paid actor playing the part of a police officer, hired by us solely to discredit Greg, then really this was becoming beyond farcical.

Paying people to pretend to be others was part of Greg's twisted games. This was his forte, we knew that only too well. Whether it be businessmen, wedding planners or even his own non-existent sister speaking to me on the phone.

If she really believed that Chris was a fake police officer who arrived at her door that August afternoon in 2017 and read Greg his rights, then how could you explain her giving a statement to the very same man at Chester-Le-Street police station only a few days later? Were Durham Police in on the plan to hoodwink her and Greg too? Could it really be part of a convoluted scam against poor old Greg? All organised by me, the vengeful, middle aged, single mum he had jilted. Hell hath no fury like a woman scorned after all. And if you then went on to delve even deeper, how could she believe Chris was fake after seeing him appear live on the national news, throughout sentencing day, giving a statement about the case, reading aloud sections of my Witness Impact statement for the world to hear?

Had we nobbled the BBC too? Got them in on the charade against Greg? Then also there was the *Love Bombed* podcast that Chris had spoken so knowledgeably on. And his appearances on the upcoming documentaries. Was this all lies too? Surely no one could be that gullible.

I rang Karen the next morning to tell her what I had learnt, and she was totally gobsmacked.

"Give me a bloody break." I could hear the annoyance in my sister's voice. "This is just laughable now. I really don't think there is any way to help that poor woman. She is beyond deluded."

I sighed down the phone. I was in complete agreement with my sister. "I know, but I can't help feeling sorry for her." I took a big swig of my coffee that had been sitting on the arm of my chair before I continued. "She must know deep down that it is a load of bull shit. She saw him plead guilty in court but she's just in too deep. She loves him and doesn't want to give up on him."

Karen agreed. "Yeah, too deep in denial."

I didn't know if it was denial on Greg's girlfriend's part, and somehow she believed his version of events. I thought it more probable that she was just too invested in their life together to face the truth. She would prefer to cut her family off, burn bridges with all of them, rather than jeopardise her fantasy life with Greg.

I heard my sister on the end of the line still speaking and I

163

forced myself out of my thoughts to concentrate on what she was saying.

"I'm sorry, this is all way too ridiculous for me. I love a bit of escapism on the telly, but this would put *The Talented Mr Ripley* to shame. I mean, fair enough when you don't know he's a lying, conniving rat. Then yeah, I get it, he can be really charming. Really seem like Mr Right. But let's face it, he's no Brad Pitt. More like a cesspit if you think about it."

I couldn't help but laugh. "Yeah, and when you know the truth all you're left with is that pathetic excuse for a man. A coward, a thief and in fact a very dangerous man. Who would willingly want that in a partner?"

Karen agreed with me. "That girl needs to give her head a wobble. She's in for a hell of a life if she doesn't wise up soon and get the hell away from him."

"I know but what can anyone do? It's her choice to stick by him. It may seem crazy to us as his victims, but it's her decision to make."

We all have choices in this life. Greg, and Greg alone, chose to do what he did to my family and friends. Lie, cheat, steal. And we had the choice to fight back. Get justice. Try to stop him doing it again and fight for some good to come from the bad.

His girlfriend, I hoped, would eventually make the right choice too.

36

Victim No More

Christmas was nearly upon us once again. Now our seventh year of festive celebrations since the shocking revelation that 'James' was in fact Greg.

The sales had really picked up for *Playing with Fire*. The book was doing so much better than we ever could have dreamed. I was now actively involved with online support groups, helping other victims, and trying to make a difference.

If only seven years ago, in those dark days, I could have known how far we would all come as a family. At that time we were in such a state of shock that I didn't know if we'd ever recover.

It was a surprise to me that I was now being approached to do live guest speaking. Me, the middle aged, unimpressive mum of three, speaking in front of large groups of people to share our story. It had been OK when it had mostly been smaller groups – I found I could cope with that pretty well. Once I got over the initial nerves, I think I did OK. Our mum would often say, if there was one thing that Karen and I could do really well, it was talk. We could blather the hind legs off a donkey. It must have been in our Irish genes.

But in a few months' time I had agreed to speak in front of an audience of over two hundred people. It was a charity event and I had asked for my fee to go directly to the charity they were supporting. That meant I could not back down as I would then be letting the charity down too. Just thinking about it though, was sending me into a panic and making my tummy lurch. I couldn't help myself; I was already a bag of nerves.

My sister had a plan for a coping strategy for me. "Just imagine them all naked and sitting constipated on the loo," she unhelpfully suggested.

I laughed at this. "Don't think that will help – it will probably just terrify me even more."

"OK, if you don't want to do that, just imagine Walter in the audience listening to every single word you say. You can get everything out; just imagine you're talking directly to him. I bet they end up having to escort you off the stage. There will be no stopping you, you'll be prattling on for hours."

I laughed at this. My sister's favoured nickname for Greg was 'Walter' as he often was compared to Walter Mitty by the entire family. She was right and I knew it deep down. I also knew I would have Karen and my mum there by my side on the day, willing me on to do well.

It certainly had been quite the emotional journey over the past few years for my family. But here we were now, out the other side, and I wasn't afraid to admit that I thought we had done bloody brilliantly. If you have a good family and support network around you, it really can make all the difference. Family is everything.

None of us asked for what Greg Wilson did to us and the pain he caused in our lives. I often get asked if I wish I could go back in time and change the past. To never go on that first date with him at that coffee shop. But what if I could create a sliding door effect? Never meet 'James', never fall in love, never have Charlie. Would I? And truthfully the answer is no. I was once asked by a stranger why I hadn't put Charlie up for adoption. How could I bear to have Greg's child and look at him every day as a constant reminder to me of what had happened? She told me it would make her sick to the stomach she would have had to get rid of him. Normally pathologically polite, on this occasion that woman got the sharp edge of my tongue. Charlie is, and always will be, the most innocent of us all. He is a wonderful blessing to our family. My proudest achievement in my life is my girls and my son. Not one of my family would change the past. None of us would be without our Charlie Bear.

37

Blast From The Past

The Christmas celebrations were in full swing. My house, normally neat and pristine, looked like a tinsel factory had exploded right in the middle of it. From being little girls Karen and I have always loved Christmas, and with Charlie being so young and a true believer in Santa Claus, I could enjoy all the festivities through the excited eyes of my little boy. Nothing is more magical.

We'd done something a little different for our family this year. We had decided to forgo the traditional turkey and have a beef joint with all the trimmings instead. Mum hadn't been pleased because she always liked to keep tradition going, but even she had to admit it had been delicious and a definite improvement on the normally dry festive bird.

I'd even decided not to bother with the Christmas pudding this year. We always had it but never really enjoyed it, and always had indigestion afterwards. This year we just relied on Mum's famous strawberry trifle – the cream and custard confection was loved by all.

Ryan was on his feet, his cheeks tinged a little pink from all the good food and even better wine.

Laura, who was wearing her reindeer antlers on top of her dyed pink hair and had been scrolling through her phone, placed it down on the dining table for her uncle's yearly toast. She nudged Katie to do the same.

Ryan cleared his throat to ensure he had everyone's attention.

"Once again that was a great meal." He nodded appreciatively at Scott. "I'm fit to burst."

Scott gestured towards the assortment of cheese, unwrapped and sitting alongside the crackers, grapes and a bottle of Port on the worktop. "We've still got my famous cheese board to go fella. I'm sure you'll be able to squeeze in a slither of cheddar or two."

Scott knew Ryan too well. He loved his cheese. But then again, we all did.

Ryan continued. "We've had a great year as a family. The best so far and hopefully even better to come. Karen and Col are well underway with their second book and I can't wait to read it soon. We're all here together despite being knocked down time and time again, and there's nowhere I'd rather be than part of this family. Here's to us all." Ryan lifted his glass. "Cheers."

We all clinked our glasses together. "Cheers."

I turned to Scott with a happy smile. "Right, now that's done, get that cheese board over here. There's always space for a bit of Stilton."

This was the first year there had been no mention of Greg. It would be his first Christmas as a free man but his shadow, so present over our family, no longer held any power over us.

I'd had such a lovely day. Laura and Katie had travelled to stay with me and Scott, as had Karen, Ryan and mum. We hadn't yet seen Scott's family, with whom I was incredibly close, but we were planning to have a second celebration with them in a few days' time, which I was really looking forward to as well. I felt so blessed to have such a wonderful extended family. They had accepted me and Charlie with such love and affection.

Later that afternoon, watching my daughters dancing around the living room swinging Charlie up in the air, much to his squeals of delight, made my heart soar. They loved their little brother so much. Earlier that day we had talked about making plans for a summer holiday together. Some family fun in the sun. I now was able to get Charlie a proper passport in his adopted name. We could travel again with no fear of awkward questions and painful explanations. I couldn't wait. It was definitely time to make some more happy memories together and get plenty of photos for our albums.

"More drinks anyone?" I looked around my family. The majority of them held their empty glasses up, keen to get a refill.

Karen passed over her vintage Babycham glass. "Another snowball for me please Col." Her face was a little flushed from the alcohol. "Not sure what's in these yellow delights but I'm betting it's not custard as it's definitely hitting the spot."

I tutted to myself. "As long as it's not hitting my carpet." I wandered around collecting all the discarded glasses. "Remember Mum's carpet back in the 80's? Nothing would shift that stain. How an innocent -looking drink could lift the pattern out of an Axminster carpet I'll never know."

I was still shaking my head as I carefully carried all the glasses back into the kitchen, trying my best to avoid them sliding off the Christmas tray. I really didn't want any rogue alcohol slopping onto my clothes. I was wearing a new red sparkly dress bought especially for the day and I felt as bright and shiny as my outfit was. I was having a perfect day.

My days of wearing drab beige cardigans and the like were well and truly behind me. I wore what I wanted now.

"Oh, I love this one," I heard Karen exclaim, as *The Killers* and *Mr Brightside* began blasting out of the Alexa in the corner of the living room. She eagerly grabbed Ryan's hand and they danced around the room together, Ryan twirling her around as she laughed.

My kids looked at them, clearly embarrassed by the oldies, and they flopped down on the sofa next to the empty piles of Quality Street wrappers and half devoured Terry's chocolate orange – normal sustenance over the festive period. Apart from the sprouts, most of the food we had consumed appeared to be brown or beige in colour. Add a few sour cream Pringles to the chocolate and that was the equivalent of a well-rounded meal at this time of year.

I busied myself in the kitchen replenishing everyone's drinks and pouring some more peanuts and snacks into the festive bowls dotted around the kitchen. They had already taken a good hammering. I really didn't know where everyone was putting it.

Earlier in the day Scott had produced a fabulous lunch. I liked to cook but he could most definitely put my culinary efforts to shame. Four courses and he didn't even break into a sweat. I would have been a frazzled gibbering wreck, but my hubby was so laid back and calm. Exactly the sort of person we needed in our lives.

As I was pouring my girls' drinks – vodka, Cherry Sourz and Cherry Pepsi Max, their preferred festive tipple – I shook my head. Even the thought of it made me feel queasy.

Mum appeared behind me in her usual festive jumper and

Christmas tree earrings and put her arms around my shoulders. "You OK love?" she questioned. "It's been such a great day, all of us here together."

I hugged her back. "I know. It's been perfect. A perfect day and the house so full of laughter."

"Splash a bit of Baileys in one of those glasses for me," she said with a little wink, and headed back to the makeshift dance floor. "I reckon Baileys is good for me. You can't have too much dairy as you get older you know," she called back over her shoulder.

And with that Mum was twisting and dancing up a storm in the middle of my lounge. Ryan had requested *A-Ha's Take On Me* on Alexa and Mum always had to dance to it, it was her favourite song. From the way she was moving and shaking I thought the calcium was doing the trick. No brittle bones there it would seem.

As I reached into the back of the fridge and located the bottle of Baileys my phone vibrated on the worktop next to the sink. I could see the recognisable blue and white logo of Facebook. I glanced over at it, expecting to see someone's family festivities or a jokey meme, but it was actually a notification of a friend request.

James Scott has sent you a friend request.

My insides turned to ice, and I nearly dropped the bottle I was holding. I tried to comprehend what was displayed on my phone's screen. It just seemed so wrong seeing his name there against the background wallpaper of Scott, me and Charlie smiling happily.

With shaking fingers I clicked on the notification message. It was the same account that had been inactive for over seven years. The account that still showed all those days when I had been with 'James' and everything we had done together.

I had a new account now and had not looked at his for years, but it was definitely the account I remembered. There were pictures of him, me, baby pictures of Charlie. All his gushing declarations of love. His lies, his deceit. All still there for everyone to see.

What the hell was going on? Why had I now had a friend request? Was Greg playing silly beggars or was he trying to hurt me all over again? Or something else?

I stared at it for what seemed like an eternity then calmly clicked 'decline' and then 'block'. Whatever the reason for him getting in touch I really didn't care. And with a smile I put my phone back down and returned to my happy family.

The people that really mattered.

The End

Also by COLEEN GREENWOOD AND KAREN CREAR

Playing with Fire: The True Story of Fireman Scam

"In my 23 years of policing, I have never encountered a man as manipulative as Greg Wilson... a compulsive liar who has shown absolutely no remorse... If somebody wrote this as a script for Coronation Street, it would be too outrageous." – Detective Constable Chris Bentham

Coleen Greenwood was overjoyed to meet James Scott, a heroic firefighter and man of her dreams. Little would she know her dreams would soon become a nightmare as his web of lies started to unravel.

The astonishing true story of one man's lies and a family's fight for justice.

This is the full untold story that was made into the BBC Sounds podcast series "Love-Bombed with Vicky Pattison" which reached No1 in the UK Apple podcasts playlist within the first week of its release.

The Reinvention of Lottie Potts

Lottie Potts is happy enough - or so she thinks. Her life is slowly ticking away as she spends her days watching old films and daydreaming about another, better, version of herself.

But Lottie isn't one for change. That is until a blonde bombshell blows into town and knocks her husband Daniel completely off his feet.

Lottie is forced to take a long hard look at herself. She is fat, in her forties and thoroughly fed up. Does she fight for her husband and the safe predictable life she knows? Or is revenge, like her favourite ice cream, a dish best served cold?

With her trusty circle of girlfriends and a surprising return from a charming face from her past, Lottie embarks on a transformative journey. Buckle up for the rollercoaster ride of laughter and tears as Lottie navigates the twists and turns of her reinvention, discovering the genuine essence of life along the way.

A portion of proceeds from sales of this book will be donated to Great Ormond Street Hospital and Epilepsy society.

Printed in Great Britain
by Amazon

38307779R00108